THE MILK SUGAR DILEMMA:

LIVING WITH LACTOSE INTOLERANCE

THE MILK SUGAR DILEMMA:

LIVING WITH LACTOSE INTOLERANCE

Richard A. Martens, M. D.

and

Sherlyn Martens, M. S., R. D.

First Printing, 1985
Second Printing, 1987, revised and expanded

Printed in the United States of America

Published by Medi-Ed Press

P.O. Box 957, East Lansing, MI 48826-0957

Cover designed by Chris Oberg

Library of Congress Cataloging in Publication Data

Martens, Richard A.
    The milk sugar dilemma: living with lactose intolerance/Richard A.
Martens, and Sherlyn Martens. -- East Lansing, Mich. :   Medi-Ed Press, 1987.
xi. 260 p. : Ill.
    1. Lactose intolerance -- Diet therapy -- Recipes. 2. Lactose intolerance
I. Martens, Sherlyn. II. Title
ISBN 0-936741-01-5
Library of Congress Catalog Card Number 85-234985

TABLE OF CONTENTS

ABOUT THE AUTHORS

Richard A. Martens, M.D., is a clinical gastroenterologist. His educational background includes DePauw and Bradley Universities, and the University of Illinois College of Medicine. Hospital training includes Evanston Hospital, Veterans Hospital, West Side, Chicago, and a Fellowship in Gastroenterology at Yale. Medical teaching appointments have included the University of Illinois, Northwestern and Loyola Universities, Chicago Medical School, the University of Hawaii, Extension Program, Ryukyu Islands, and Michigan State University. Practice experience includes Illinois, U. S. Army, Connecticut and Massachusetts. Since 1970, he has been in East Lansing, Michigan, in private medical practice limited to consultative gastroenterology.

Sherlyn Martens, M.S., R.D., clinical nutritionist, has completed undergraduate and graduate work at Michigan State University, and has published an instructional unit on nutritional counseling used in the education of dietetic students. She has worked in many environments from nursing homes to hospitals from Michigan to Louisiana. Formerly involved in teaching, hospital and private dietetic counseling, she currently limits herself to nutritional consultation for Gastroenterology Associates of East Lansing, Michigan.

FOREWORD

Who among us has not felt totally inferior in some field of endeavor? While I consider myself a reasonably scholarly sort, well-educated and experienced in my chosen area of medicine, I must admit that I know relatively little about anything else. Professionals of all stripes are skilled at making us all feel inadequate. The great country philosopher Will Rogers once said: "Everybody is ignorant, only on different subjects."

Most areas are unnecessarily confusing today. Physicians and lawyers, among others, continuously complicate tasks beyond the level required. They obfuscate otherwise simple things in the interest of appearances. When we finished this book, for instance, we inquired of an attorney how one should proceed to copyright it. He noted that it was likely that no one locally could handle it. He told us of an attorney formerly in copyright law who was employed by the State of Michigan, and suggested that he might help us. When contacted, that attorney noted that the document, when printed, is effectively copyrighted. Only if we planned to sue someone was it likely to be necessary to have the documents on file. Further, it would be improbable that anyone would blatantly plagiarize our work because of the risk of copyright infringement. Nevertheless, he advised that the documents be filed, and forwarded them to us. He assured us that anyone with a grammar school education could fill out the forms. It proved to be no more complex than an application for a library card.

Personal suspicions about the propriety and acceptance of the label, and the refusal of my wife and colleagues in this endeavor to agree, are all that prevent entitling this work: *Lactose Intolerance, for Idiots*. Without calumny intended, it is hoped that this text simplifies this complex subject sufficiently that the reader can understand it, even enjoy it, without having to consult other references. This has been our goal!

Richard A. Martens, M.D.

PREFACE

Lactose intolerance is not the same as milk allergy. Indeed, it has nothing to do with allergy. The symptoms are related to the inability to digest lactose, the sugar naturally present in the milk of mammals. The problem is frequently overlooked, commonly misdiagnosed and usually underestimated since it is rarely a nutritional problem. All too often the symptoms of lactose intolerance are incorrectly attributed to "stress." Clients are advised that they are "too sensitive," the implication being that they're "a little nuts," and they are told that they should learn to live with a little adversity!

With varying symptoms and frequency, in varying degrees of severity, lactose intolerance affects about sixty million people in North America, and an equal or greater number in Europe. Without doubt it is fortunate that the problem is not commonly severe or nutritionally important. As will be seen, however, one can advance the argument that *people who tolerate lactose are the unusual ones.* Intolerance to lactose is likely the commonest cause of diarrhea and/or gaseousness in man. It is especially troublesome in western civilizations where dairy products are ritually accepted as a necessary nutrient--even the perfect food. Further, as European and North American cultures tend to depend more on prepared or convenience foods, wherein lactose in some form is a common additive, the problem becomes increasingly relevant.

This text explains this lactose intolerance in non-medical language. Hopefully the book will familiarize the afflicted with its dietary management, and be recommended and used by professionals in counseling their patients. It offers a discussion which is informative, and a dietary program which is understandable, varied, balanced and satisfying. Nutritional tables are comprehensive and were created by the authors (from basic sources) for this book. The final sections are dedicated to the provision of recipes, menus, and hints on food preparation sufficiently detailed to interest and satisfy even a novice cook.

It should be emphasized that *five to ten percent of persons so afflicted have an underlying disease with which lactose intolerance is associated. We caution these people to seriously consider medical evaluation to rule out the possibility of an intestinal disease with lactose intolerance, as opposed to primary lactose intolerance; especially so if their response to the diet is incomplete.*

We also caution professionals to recall that maldigestion of one substance may imply maldigestion or malabsorption of others; that maldigestion and malabsorption are generally symptoms, not diseases; that these facts may bode ill for the person in whom the basic disease process is overlooked. That said, however, this text should alert all with lactose intolerance to the problem and offer satisfactory answers for its management, regardless of cause.

A warning is offered agencies of generous governments of the western world, and to persons of philanthropic persuasion in the same societies. For those who would, for humanitarian reasons, rush many lactose-laden products to the starving of the "underdeveloped world," it must be noted that these could be more of a problem than a solution.

This monograph is not intended to be a definitive treatise on the subject. The interested reader or academician is directed to a superb text: *LACTOSE DIGESTION: Clinical and Nutritional Implications;* D.M. Paige, M.D., & T.M. Bayless, M.D., editors; The Johns Hopkins University Press, 1981. This scholarly work explores the subject in detail, listing numerous references including many of the more than 1700 research and clinical papers dealing with this and related subjects.

While much has been written in the medical literature, this problem had escaped discussion in a lay text. The first edition of this book rectified that situation. The second edition is possible because of an increased awareness by food manufacturers, as well as their willingness to permit publication of additional information, which greatly enhances the food product section of this volume. This offered an opportunity to re-edit the information to render it more readable, while maintaining simplicity and practicality. We feel that the new edition will better help those who suffer from this malady to adapt to their required dietary restriction; and that it will do so in a fashion which is acceptable, satisfying, and productive of symptomatic relief without compromising good nutrition or health.

1

LACTOSE INTOLERANCE

For every person aware that his symptoms are due to lactose intolerance there are likely ten others who do not know, and suffer because they do not know. Of all the people who think they follow a lactose-free diet, only one in ten actually does. They are unaware that a lactose-free diet and milk-free diet are not the same thing!

A CASE HISTORY

Fifteen years ago when I (RAM) was in practice in New England, a frustrated, depressed 40-year-old man was referred to me. He had experienced loose stools several times daily for many years, but for the two prior years he simply could not remove himself from the house because of violent, sometimes incontinent diarrhea. He commonly experienced twenty to thirty gassy explosive diarrheal stools per day. They were so urgent that he was literally chained to the lavatory. If he had to go somewhere, he could not eat for at least twelve hours before the outing. He was the sole support of his wife and four children. While formerly hard working, productive and successful, he had not worked for over two years.

He had been evaluated repeatedly, having numerous

diagnostic tests and many trials of diet and medication. Thousands of dollars had been spent on physicians, tests and drugs. Despite the most potent of the diarrhea medications, he continued to have as many as twenty stools per day.

Among other things, he had been advised to follow a bland diet. Such diets are considered by physicians to be the very best for sick people. (Even the dictionary agrees, defining bland as: "non-irritating, non-stimulating, and soothing.") A bland diet usually consists of milk products in large quantities and other foods which are "pleasantly gentle and agreeable." No one, including the patient, noted that he worsened as he more rigidly adhered to his bland diet.

After many months of therapy, his psychiatrist finally gave up on him. He considered the man intractably neurotic, obsessed by some compulsion to avoid work, using diarrhea as his excuse. This, despite a twenty-year work history, home ownership, and status as a productive citizen supporting a wife and children.

He had been everywhere. Answers were not forthcoming. He considered himself mentally ill, since no one could find anything wrong. While he didn't know why he was "sick in the head," there was nothing else to believe. Tests had clearly shown that there was no medical problem. In total frustration he came, indicating that if he could not be helped he would probably commit suicide. At least then he'd be out of his misery. Though unemployed for over two years, he could not qualify for welfare since he owned his home. His debts had mounted, and he had remortgaged his home to pay his bills. His wife's ability to work was limited because of her own health problems and her obligations to their children. He was and had always been the breadwinner. Now he wasn't working. He couldn't!

Though by itself disabling, his only complaint was gassy diarrhea. There was no fever, weight loss, or any real sense of sickness. Nevertheless, he was "sick-and-tired of being sick-and-tired." There were no other symptoms. He had been comprehensively studied by legions of physicians throughout New England, thus it seemed pointless to repeat the tests. After only a few minutes time to review his history and perform a simple physical exam, I suggested that he first try a *lactose-free diet,* and eliminate all medications. He had never heard of a lactose-free diet. He intimated that *I* was the crazy one. It couldn't be *that* simple! His desperation was such, however, that he decided he would try anything--once.

The next day he called to report that he had experienced no diarrhea for twenty-four hours. He was very surprised, and pleased--and hopeful, as well. That had been the first day in over ten years during which he had had *no* stools. He returned to my office in tears a week later, thankful that his life had been restored to him. He had returned to work, promptly, on his second day without diarrhea; returned after two years of being unable to go to work at all.

This case history is extreme, without doubt, though I have seen others nearly as severe. They do emphasize a point: there are literally thousands of people in the western world just, or nearly, like him, and there are hundreds of thousands who suffer less. All suffer unnecessarily, most in silence, having been assured that "nothing is wrong."

THE ORIGIN OF LACTOSE INTOLERANCE

There exists a singular and unique intestinal enzyme, lactase, which is necessary to digest the chemical bond between the simple sugars glucose and galactose, which together form lactose. This sugar is found naturally in all mammalian milk and in most products derived from it. When there is a deficiency or absence of *lactase*, the ability of the intestine to digest *lactose* is compromised. This influences the ability of the afflicted person to tolerate this sugar in his diet. (Various aspects of this problem are discussed separately throughout this book.)

Lactose intolerance occurs in three basic forms. The first, **congenital**, is rare, and limited to newborns. The second, **primary acquired**, is by far the most common, and appears after the weaning period. The third, **secondary acquired,** can result from many diseases, treatment with certain drugs, and some kinds of surgery. *The result, regardless of cause, is a varying combination of symptoms which include rumbling, bloating, gaseousness, flatulence, cramping, and diarrhea.*

Discussed in this section is the incidence of the problem, along with a description of the origin and nature of lactose intolerance. Explanations of the events give the reader a clear idea why these symptoms occur. In lay terms, it provides a scientific basis upon which to understand and learn to live with lactose intolerance. Also included are other case examples to illustrate common presentations, descriptions of the diagnostic tests, and discussion of other considerations relevant to those who experience symptoms from this malady.

CONGENITAL LACTOSE INTOLERANCE

The **genetic** form is rare since it is basically self-destructive. If a child is born unable to digest milk sugar, he is deprived of any source of nutrition for weeks, which is incompatible with life. Usually it is not just lactose which the infant cannot digest, but also maltose and sucrose. Today, these infants can be fed alternate, soybean or synthetic, disaccharide-free formulas. Many survive in western nations because of medical sophistication. We now know that most of these infants outgrow the problem within weeks or months. Formerly this could not be determined, since they all died before they outgrew it. Since it is more common in premature infants it may become more common as more of these "premies" survive, mature, and pass-it-along.

PRIMARY ACQUIRED
LACTOSE INTOLERANCE

This variant is also **genetic** and seems to be a programmed phenomenon. It is by far the most common form of lactose intolerance. In fact it is the dominant condition in humans. Below are the facts, and an hypothesis which might help to explain why this is so.

Facts: The ability to digest milk sugar peaks during the second or third day after birth and declines slowly thereafter. Lactase levels are ordinarily very high during infancy because lactose is ingested in very large quantities. Nursing, or equivalents, continue as the primary source of nutrition. Lactase levels wane during weaning and begin to disappear as other foods are introduced. The enzyme is nearly gone when the "outside diet" is sufficient. When weaning is complete, the production of the enzyme simply stops, or is greatly reduced. This occurs spontaneously: a genetically preconditioned shut-off common to the vast majority of humans. The capability to digest lactose is significantly compromised by the second or third year of life, except in selected populations (i.e., in groups where natural selection has favored lactose tolerance). Thus, all pre-adolescents of mammalian species acquire lactose intolerance at an early age. The use of lactose thereafter does not force the production of the enzyme; it simply produces gas and diarrhea. Except in its fermented form, milk is poorly tolerated by most humans, everafter.

Hypothesis: Eons ago, "Mother Nature" undertook to provide a means for the termination of suckling in pre-adolescent mammals, to permit creation of new progeny and to allow the new infants to survive. This also forced more wide-ranging dietary habits necessary to survival, growth and maturity of the older young. Natural selection either favored this change, or did not permit its alteration. By providing for the gradual decline in lactase levels, nature offered encouragement to seek alternate food sources. It wisely allowed for the very young to develop the skill to find foods other than milk, by continuing lactation and permitting suckling, in a process called weaning. When one offspring was self-sufficient, nature allowed conception of another. With new young, however, and the return of lactation, there was assurance that the stronger, older young would not return to the breast. Nature arranged that they would be made uncomfortable by it, thus allowing survival of the infant while forcing normal growth and development of the adolescent.

In mammals the subtraction of milk as a sustaining food clearly doesn't impact on survival. Indeed, since it is nutritionally inadequate for adults, the continued use of milk may be a detriment. Other sources of food take the place of milk. So it is with most of mankind. (This does not imply that milk is bad. Milk *is* an excellent resource when it is tolerated, and it certainly facilitates good nutrition.)

In primitive "gathering" non-dairying cultures, the critical nutritional content of milk is replaced by the consumption of large quantities of grubs, greens, mushrooms and nuts. Farming in primitive cultures permits a more varied and predictable diet, as do hunting and herding. Ages ago some herding cultures determined that the preparation of what we know as yogurt preserved milk for a month or more. It provided a nutritious product which could be both stored and consumed by adults for nutrition. The males of Asian steppe cultures regularly consumed fermented mares' milk as an alcoholic beverage, though by virtue of their Oriental heritage they are lactose-intolerant, by definition. In riparian and seafaring (those near, and dependent on lakes, rivers or oceans) non-dairying societies, nutrition is adequate because of the regular use of fish, bone meal, rice, kelp and sprouts, as well as greens, mushrooms and nuts.

As man adapted culture to his environment he was able to slowly determine what constituted good nutrition. Archæology provides ample evidence for the existence of very well-balanced diets, designed by observation and instinct, in cultures which were old ten thousand years ago.

INCIDENCE OF LACTOSE INTOLERANCE

Any discussion of the incidence is limited to primary acquired lactose intolerance, a recessive genetic trait occurring primarily in cultures where milk is not used for food after weaning (or is used only in fermented forms: e.g., yogurt). Secondary intolerance is much less common than primary, and meaningful statistics are not available to reflect the proportion of total cases which it represents.

Unexplained diarrhea and/or gaseousness, especially when it occurs daily, is progressive throughout waking hours, or meal-related, should be considered probably caused by lactose ntolerance until disproved. It is even more likely the case if there has been a recent intestinal infection or infestation with parasites, recent use of antibiotics or treatment with cancer drugs, or a history of ulcer surgery, inflammatory bowel disease, intestinal resection, celiac disease or sprue. It is virtually certain if the afflicted person is black, Oriental, Indian, Mediterranean, Jewish, Mexican, American Indian or of other native New World descent (North, Central, or South American).

The table below, reproduced on the back cover, recants the approximate incidence of this phenomenon.

Incidence of Lactose Intolerance in Adults

Ethnic Group	% Intolerant
African blacks	97 -100
Dravidian Indians (India)	95 -100
Orientals	90 -100
North American Indians	80 - 90
Central/South American Indians	70 - 90
Mexican Americans	70 - 80
North American blacks	70 - 75
Mediterraneans	60 - 90
Jews	60 - 80
Central & Northern Indians (India)	25 - 65
Middle Europeans	10 - 20
North American Caucasians	7 - 15
Northwestern Indians (India/Pakistan)	3 - 15
Northern Europeans	1 - 5

As is clear from the above statistics, the vast majority of humans on earth do not tolerate milk sugar. In the following pages on lactose intolerance, directed towards the North American and western European reader, we are discussing as *abnormal* a situation which is the usual state in the human population at large. When reviewing the subject from the standpoint of ethnic origin, *the normal, non-Caucasian adult is lactose-intolerant!* Since intolerance to lactose is genetic, there is little hope (nor is there evidence) that the systematic use of this sugar in one's diet will stimulate the ability to digest it. Experiments have proven that *the use of lactose will not increase tolerance.*

Genetic tolerance to lactose seems to have emerged in the dairying cultures of eastern Eurasia which originated five to ten thousand years ago. Dairying became common and spread widely to northern Europe, parts of Africa and the Indian subcontinent. It was transported by eastern Mediterranean emigrants and incorporated into new cultures. *Natural selection and survival in those groups favored individuals in whom lactose tolerance existed.* This fostered the predominance of an unusual lactose tolerant breed of people. Since the migrants were "white," the ability to tolerate lactose is an almost uniquely Caucasian trait! In fact, in the black and Indian populations of the Americas (and India), there is a direct correlation between the ratio of "white blood" and the ability of persons of mixed heritage to tolerate lactose. The indigenous west African blacks have a near 100% inability to digest lactose. The blacks in America are almost exclusively of west African descent, yet (because of their 30% interracial derivation) have a 25-30% ability to tolerate lactose. This is true of the American Indian populations studied, as well. Lactose intolerance in Mexicans is estimated to be in the range of 75%, reflecting their interracial derivation as a Caucasian/Spanish admixture dating from the conquistadors. To our knowledge, studies of other native Central and South American populations are not available, but one would expect the same statistics to prevail. The same incidence applies to the Indo-European population of northern India and Pakistan, materially influenced by ancient Aryan migration.

Contrariwise, the indigenous Dravidian population of eastern and southern India (and Bangladesh) remains lactose-intolerant. The ability to tolerate lactose in the Indian subcontinent can be roughly predicted by measuring the distance removed from the original Indus Valley culture, the ancient Indo-Aryan population center in northwestern India (now Pakistan). It is noteworthy that selected dairying tribes from "Black Africa" have a greater than 90% ability to tolerate lactose, as do the Caucasian populations of western Europe and North America. On the other hand, though of Caucasian origin, Laplanders have a 25-60% inability to digest milk sugar, presumably because they began dairying only a few hundred years ago.

SECONDARY LACTOSE INTOLERANCE

On **non-genetic** bases, lactose intolerance is known to appear in most all people with untreated celiac disease (an intestinal problem due to gluten sensitivity), up to half of the individuals diagnosed as having inflammatory bowel diseases (Crohn's disease, ulcerative colitis, etc.), numerous persons with small-intestinal parasites (Giardia Lamblia, hookworm, etc.), in many with pancreatic insufficiency (due to cystic fibrosis or alcoholism) and others with more exotic diseases (immunologic deficiency states, tropical sprue, and kwashiorkor among them). It commonly complicates infectious diarrhea, and can result from treatment with antibiotics and cancer drugs. Malnutrition of any origin is yet another cause.

The most frequent single cause is intestinal (usually viral) infection. The first symptoms of secondary lactose intolerance are often experienced during or following such an illness. Not rarely, adults become ill from an intestinal infection, recover from the headache, fatigue, exhaustion, fever and nausea, only to find themselves bothered by persisting diarrhea and gaseousness which will not subside. This tendency often becomes worse after subsequent infections and with increasing age.

All of the causes mentioned above are in some fashion related to shortening cell life or compromising cell function of the small-intestinal cells. These manufacture lactase, which in turn digests the lactose (all of which is more fully discussed in SECTION 2). While some of these may reflect other genetic traits, the primary process seems to be different, and treatment or resolution of the problem, or elimination of the drug is often noted to restore tolerance to lactose over a period of time.

There are other situations in which lactase may not be reduced; rather, its effectiveness is compromised. In this group of people the symptoms occur as a result of insufficient exposure of the small-intestinal cells to the food products, either because of rapid transit through the intestine (as in the dumping syndrome associated with ulcer surgery), removal of the intestine (resection for disease), or exclusion of intestine (as with the by-pass operation formerly done for obesity).

OTHER CASE EXAMPLES

CASE NUMBER ONE: About three years ago I (RAM) was asked to evaluate a single 35-year-old male Caucasian high school teacher. He told me he was troubled after meals with gassy, diarrheal stools that increased as the day wore on. The symptoms were worse in the late evening after dinner. Being a bachelor, he frequented the neighborhood fast-food establishments, and otherwise lived "out of the convenience departments" of the local grocery. He stopped for breakfast at a local diner, ate lunch at the school cafeteria, and went to a nearby hamburger stop for dinner. If he ate at home, his specialty was the microwaved frozen pot pie. He had virtually never cooked a "scratch meal" in his life.

The gassy diarrhea was most inconvenient and quite disturbing to him. In frustration he had tried many suggestions to correct it. All were to no avail. He decided to travel the considerable distance to my office for another opinion. Having had numerous tests prior to coming to me, he was not subjected to further study. The history was classic and his response to the lactose-restricted trial diet was gratifying, if not complete: his gaseousness was considerably reduced and his diarrhea disappeared. Sustained response did require considerable and continuing adherence to the dietary program.

For more than a year he did quite well; though, looking back, he was never completely free of symptoms. His satisfaction and his continuing response were sufficient to dissuade me, and him, from consideration of further assessment. Over a two-year interval he gradually noted a return of the loose stools, and mild increase in gaseousness. Minor drug therapy and the restriction of a few more foods again relieved his symptoms.

Finally, however, he again worsened, though there were no new symptoms. There was nothing to suggest a serious disease, but because of his symptomatic recurrence during treatment I advised that he be further studied. All of the blood chemistries and stool tests were normal, as was the repeat barium enema X-ray of his colon. Colonoscopy (direct examination) was undertaken. This revealed very mild, but definite, involvement of the bowel by ulcerative colitis (one of the inflammatory bowel diseases), treatment for which has completely reversed all symptomatology. With response of his colitis to sulfa, his lactose tolerance actually improved a little. He has nevertheless been shown to have a potentially serious disease which must be observed, treated and kept under control.

In similar fashion one could report on cases of celiac disease, Giardiasis, pancreatic insufficiency, etc., diagnosed as a result of further assessment after failure of response to a lactose-free program. Alternatively, one could report on cases of recognized diseases which did not respond to appropriate primary therapy until lactose restriction was added.

CASE NUMBER TWO: "Then there's the one about" the sixty-year-old professor who had ulcers for years. He didn't always do everything right, but he had managed to maintain himself in a relatively symptom-free state for years by using milk products every few hours. He became such a devotee that he drank a half-gallon of milk daily while using other milk products as well. He really "loved them." When introduced to an arthritic drug his ulcers worsened, hemorrhage occurred, and he required an operation to stop the bleeding and "fix" his ulcer.

Subsequently he developed what is known as a "dumping syndrome," which is very common with people after ulcer surgery. Any amount of milk consumed would produce gas, and any satisfying amount would produce diarrhea. He was devastated! Not only were the symptoms miserable, he had to give up his favorite beverage and everything made from it--foods he had come to prefer during the many years of "nursing his ulcer." However, even after putting himself on a *milk-free* diet, he was far from free of the bothersome symptoms. There were times he wished he had his ulcer back.

Various medicines had been tried. While some relieved

the diarrhea they made him more miserable because of gas retention and bloating. He was referred for nutritional counseling, and introduced to a *lactose-restricted* anti-dumping program. He was able to stop all of his medications. He couldn't drink a lot of milk but he could use it in small amounts and he could satisfy his preferences by using many things made from it. (In the latter portion of this book you will find many of these helpful suggestions.)

WHY DID LACTOSE TOLERANCE APPEAR?

Lactose tolerance is exhibited in adults of dairying cultures wherein the use of milk, in an unaltered form, continues throughout life. The exact reasons for its dominance and impact on survival are not clear. It could be that in times of famine, milk was the only ready source of food. Those who could tolerate it fared better, reproduced more frequently or more effectively, and eventually prevailed in these cultures. Perhaps because of milk, good nutrition was a little easier to achieve, and those who could tolerate it were genetically favored. Finally, it might have been that in a dairying culture, sooner or later, those who could benefit from the produce of that society tended to predominate.

Regardless, it can be statistically proved that over a period of 5000 years a 3% survival advantage from a given genetic trait will result in the existence of that trait in almost 100% of that population. This appears to be the case with lactose tolerance, irrespective of the reasons.

SYMPTOMS OF LACTOSE INTOLERANCE

Because of this digestive problem, lactose is not absorbed from the small intestine and soon reaches the large intestine or colon. The colon harbors bacteria that normally eek out a spartan existence rummaging through leftover dietary fiber. Offered the chance, these bacteria instantly ferment lactose into organic acids and carbon dioxide. The organic acids are quickly absorbed from the colon, resulting in the recovery of most of the calories; thus important nutritional consequence is prevented. The carbon dioxide, however, results in bloating, and often in immediate "gas pains." Lactose carries with it into the colon large volumes of water in which it is dissolved, and other electrolytes dissolved in the water. Together the gas and liquid cause overactivity of the intestine, and when the colon is overloaded, it promptly expels this excess fluid as diarrhea. (Though rare, severe diarrhea can result in electrolyte depletion and dehydration.)

Problems often occur within minutes after the ingestion of large volumes of lactose. They can appear many hours later, however. Symptoms usually include the above-mentioned abdominal bloating or distress, overactivity and cramping, gaseousness and diarrhea. Sometimes there is associated pain, and not rarely there is incontinence of stool (lack of control, with accidental evacuation). Some of these symptoms occur in all patients with lactose intolerance. The existence of any of them should raise the question of this problem. The combination of all of them practically assures the diagnosis.

DIAGNOSIS OF LACTOSE INTOLERANCE

For all but research purposes, the diagnosis of simple lactose intolerance is a clinical one. *When adherence to a lactose-free diet results in the disappearance of symptoms, that is sufficient to confirm it.* If other serious considerations are absent, no other testing is required. If symptoms are incompletely eliminated, or if there is a suspicion of other problems, further testing should be carried out.

The principal specific test used to confirm the existence of this problem is known as the **lactose tolerance test.** It is performed in a fashion quite similar to the glucose tolerance test, diagnostic for diabetes mellitus. The test involves the consumption of 50 grams of lactose (approximately the amount in a quart of milk), after which the blood sugar is measured at 30, 60, 90, and 120 minutes. A rise in the blood sugar of more than 20 milligrams is considered normal, and theoretically rules out lactose intolerance. However, in diabetic persons who clear the sugar from the blood more slowly than usual, and in others who empty their stomachs more slowly than usual, the results are erratic and can confuse the diagnosis. Hence, even *the* diagnostic test is not always accurate, and *observation of the response to the consumption of the lactose is helpful--even necessary.*

Since organic acids are a by-product of lactose fermentation in the colon, **measuring stool acidity** (by testing with litmus paper, or other means) can be helpful in corroborating the diagnosis. **Measuring stool sugar** (by chemical analysis or the use of Clinitest tablets) can also be useful. Since there is too much variability in adults, these tests are of value only in children, and then are often considered unreliable.

The newer **breath hydrogen test** (H_2 test) is considered by many to be the most accurate of the clinically available studies to confirm lactose intolerance. Furthermore, it has the capability of approximating the level of lactose intolerance. Hydrogen is produced only by bacteria in the colon, and only if they have access to a sugar. After hydrogen is produced in the colon, it is absorbed into the bloodstream and carried to lungs where it is exhaled. Hence, a measured amount of lactose can be given, the expired air collected, and the hydrogen content measured and compared to the dose of lactose. The amount of hydrogen expelled correlates quite closely with the level of lactose maldigestion, and therefore intolerance.

The definitive proof of the diagnosis rests with the **biochemical determination of lactase deficiency** on analysis of tissue homogenate (i.e., one must obtain a fairly large, very fresh piece of intestinal lining, grind it up, and perform critical, chemical analysis for the enzyme, lactase, and demonstrate that the level is lower than the expected normal). This test is available only in large and special centers, only for research purposes, and only at enormous cost. Hence it is not a clinically useful tool in an ordinary practice application.

THE TROUBLE WITH TESTS

The problem with testing is that it is *unreliable or unpredictable* in many situations, and *too* scientific in others. In all, it can be clinically inadequate or inaccurate. Some people who are lactose-intolerant are only intolerant of large volumes of lactose, and not intolerant enough to measure, though they are still symptomatic. The ability to measure is then of no real benefit to the patient. Others are highly sensitive to the ingestion of this sugar. A number of these people may not have truly dramatic intolerance when measured, yet the problems are severe. Symptoms often far outweigh even the clinically measurable gas and diarrhea. Either because of truly profound intolerance, extreme intestinal sensitivity, or a very low threshold to pain, some people get severe symptoms from tiny amounts of this product. A skeptical scientist might note that "the measurable intolerance to lactose is not that striking." Hence, there is the implication that the afflicted individual is either exaggerating or prevaricating. That's not necessarily so. Irrespective of the ability to test the intolerance, some people can recognize the ingestion of as little as a gram of lactose (less than the amount in 2 tablespoonsful of milk) even though they didn't know it was there!

THE DO-IT-YOURSELF TEST

The **lactose challenge** and the **lactose-free test** are the only two practical and readily available means of assessment for lactose intolerance. The finest physician has little more that is clinically useful at his disposal. If the symptoms include only gas and diarrhea; if there is no weight loss, bleeding, or fever; and if there are no symptoms to suggest a more serious problem, a case can be made for not wasting the time or funds necessary to get tests done. There is far too much of this unnecessary "study." Patients shouldn't insist on tests that their physicians feel are wasteful; physicians shouldn't suggest tests which are unnecessary. Needless tests are unduly costly, and not much fun, either.

LACTOSE CHALLENGE: By consuming a quart of dairy milk at one sitting, preferably over no more than 15 minutes, one can determine whether or not he is lactose-intolerant. (Skim milk or 2% milk is preferable because of the effect of fat on stomach emptying.) If within minutes or hours, the subject experiences diarrhea and/or bloating he can be sure he is intolerant. This test is easily accomplished at a cost of seventy cents, instead of seventy (or seven hundred) dollars. It can be done when convenient rather than on a workday morning in a laboratory during otherwise productive time.

LACTOSE-FREE TEST: Abstinence from lactose for five days resulting in the disappearance of symptoms is just as diagnostic. This approach is especially recommended when an individual is already aware that he is intolerant to milk. While not likely to seriously affect one's health, a quart of milk can produce real misery in a profoundly intolerant person.

In either of the above tests the establishment of the existence of lactose intolerance should be fairly clear. The question remaining is: "*how* intolerant?" This is not answered by the conventional medical tests, either. Establishing one's individual tolerance is not that difficult. See SECTION 5.

CAUSES FOR CONCERN

For more complex cases, or when response to a lactose-free diet is incomplete, further testing is indicated. In persons with complaints of fever, weight loss, bleeding and the like, continuation of a lactose-free diet is recommended while other studies are completed. Chemical analyses of the blood, X-ray studies of the intestine, endoscopy and intestinal biopsy may be necessary. Studies of distant organs may be reasonable. These situations require the attention of a physician and the concerned individual is advised to seek it. A note of caution is required to avoid overlooking a serious disease:

While lactose intolerance is generally a bothersome symptom, it can be a signal of another disease. Medical evaluation is best if there is any question, or if the response to diet is incomplete. Talk to your physician if you are not well.

CONCLUSION

For a variety of reasons, lactose intolerance occurs with varying symptoms and frequency, in varying degrees of severity, in well over sixty million North Americans. Till proven otherwise, meal related, daily, progressive gaseousness must be presumed due to lactose intolerance, as must gassy diarrhea. This is especially true if the afflicted person is not Caucasian; if there has been a history of recent intestinal infection or parasite; if antibiotics or cancer drugs have been used; if he is known to have had ulcer surgery, bowel resection, intestinal by-pass, inflammatory bowel disease, pancreatic problems, or celiac sprue; if he is immune-deficient, malnourished or otherwise digestively compromised.

COUNTERPOINT

Since lactose intolerance is the usual adult state, and especially in the "third world," policy planners of this world should be advised to heed some of the considerations in this manual. As prepared foods, western tastes and habits are increasingly adopted by developing nations, care should be taken to avoid problems. It is this group of people who, by all counts, represent the majority of lactose-intolerant humans on the planet. Certain nutritional concepts, production techniques, and food fetishes of the "advanced West" can be counter-productive, even devastating, in other parts of the globe. Especially since the intolerance to lactose is genetic, there is little hope that its systematic use will stimulate the ability to digest it--at least not in one lifetime. While there can be little doubt that those who tolerate this sugar have developed genetically in such a way as to permit it, it would be foolhardy to overlook the fact that it took at least 5000 years to accomplish this feat, and "good intentions" had nothing to do with it.

LIVING WITH LACTOSE INTOLERANCE

Simple milk avoidance can result in reduction or disappearance of the symptoms; however, this would result in a diet deficient in calcium, and is not recommended. Compliance with a lactose-restricted diet is far more confusing. Understanding the essentials makes that accommodation less bewildering, but it does not make it a simple program. A lactose-restricted diet is difficult without guidance, but the rewards of study and instruction can be satisfaction, comfort, and a much more varied diet.

Many food products such as bread and cake mixes have milk solids added as a part of their manufacture. In a variety of cream soups, dressings and canned meats, the determination of the presence of milk powder may be difficult. In all, the presence of lactose may be noted only as an afterthought in the fine print on the label. Lactose, unlike flour or cornstarch, is an ideal commercial thickener for soups, gravies, sauces, etc. It dissolves instantly, and doesn't lump. Convenience products often incorporate lactose to facilitate ease of commercial production, and to improve the appearance, texture, acceptance and marketability of the product. Whey (a lactose-laden milk by-product of cheese manufacture) is similarly added--sometimes in large quantities. Since lactose assists in dissolving powdered substances, it is often used in drink mixes, dried foods, and "instant" products. It frequently appears in some form in frozen convenience dinners. Since lactose is not very sweet, unlike cane or beet sugar, it is a useful thickener for packaged fruits and juices, and in desserts and liqueurs as well. It provides "body" while avoiding unwanted sweetness. Finally, when exposed to water, lactose quickly expands. This physical property is used to explode tablets and assists in the more rapid absorption of drugs following their ingestion. It is a substance common to many vitamins and medications sold in tablet form. Fortunately there is so little lactose in most tablets that it rarely presents a problem. A notable exception is in people with severe lactose intolerance who take large doses of Vitamin C.

As is apparent from these final paragraphs, some direction is clearly necessary in order to follow a lactose-restricted diet. To the extent that this program makes any sense, the "logic" must be derived from a knowledge of where lactose is likely to be found. For many people with this intolerance, a majority of convenience foods may be denied, and a return to "scratch cooking" may be necessary. Arguably, however, this is at once more nutritious, less expensive, and better for one's health.

Following, then, is a comprehensive assessment and explanation of the syndrome of lactose intolerance and its management. To the best of our ability it is reduced to lay terminology. We hope this will make it available to everyone interested in the subject, without compromising content. Most diets are a technical series of "don'ts." We have tried to explain the problems and possibilities to make this diet a program of "do's."

After careful study of this manual--with a little practice and patience--the reader will find it comfortable to purchase, prepare, and consume flavorful satisfying well-balanced meals which are nutritious and appealing. Most will find that selected milk products are well tolerated if the right choices are made. All should benefit dramatically from symptomatic relief.

2

DIGESTION

GENERALITIES

Digestion of food is quite complex. The digestive sequence results in the step-by-step reduction of raw food into its elements.

The process begins in the mouth. The teeth might be compared to a cleaver, coarsely chopping material into finer pieces; the enzymes compared to the knife, carefully separating the material into its component parts. Chewing grinds food into smaller pieces while mixing it with the saliva. Saliva adds water for dilution and enzymes which begin digestion. Some starches are started on the road to destruction by chewing and mixing with salivary amylases. The food is then swallowed and passed from the mouth, through the esophagus, quickly into the stomach.

The stomach is basically a blender which, by muscular contraction, continues to mulch the food when it arrives there. Large quantities of water, acid and other enzymes are added to the food in the stomach, diluting it to about the same density as body fluid while contributing further to its destruction. When properly thinned, mixed and pulverized, the food exits the stomach through the pyloric valve into the duodenum (the first portion of the small intestine).

The elements are absorbed from the small intestine and distributed throughout the body to its various organs and structures where many of these fractions are further transformed within the cells of the body for use. Just as the butcher dismembers the inedible portions of animal carcasses into steaks, chops, fillets and roasts for food, so does digestion "render" proteins, starches and fats into their smallest usable fragments to provide energy and the essentials for health, growth and development. (See illustration.)

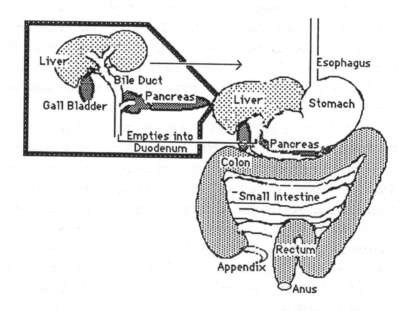

As shown in the illustration, in the duodenum are ducts leading from the liver and the pancreas. These ducts deliver enzymes (from the pancreas) and bile (from the liver) into the duodenum where they are mixed with the food to further its digestion.

The pancreatic enzymes are numerous and varied. The many peptidases break down proteins; lipases break down fats; amylases break down starches; and so on. Most foods have a designated pattern of digestion, with special enzymes responsible for specific portions of this pattern.

The small intestine has other enzymes, in addition to catalysts which accelerate the processes of digestion. Many of the nutrients considered essential in the human diet are necessary because of special requirements of the digestive process. Without them the systems will not work.

The whole scheme is marvelously complex and intricately interdependent. Despite the efforts of research, the sequence is still not well understood; experts change their minds from time to time as more information becomes available. A brief outline of digestion follows, with a more complete discussion of sugars, focusing on lactose.

As noted, digestion is responsible for the reduction of foods to elemental forms usable by the body. Dietary proteins, represented by meats, some vegetables and nuts, have complex linkages which are reduced by proteases to their smaller portions, and by specific peptidases into their smallest units. At their simplest, the proteins are made of amino acids, the building blocks of human protein. Some are essential amino acids. As mortar is essential to a solid brick wall, so are certain amino acids essential to viable human proteins. See illustration on the following page.

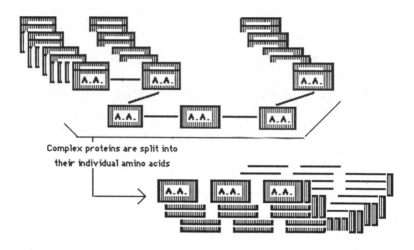

Complex proteins are split into
their individual amino acids

Fat digestion is slower than that of other energy-producing nutrients. It is slower in part because it is more complex, in part because fat is not soluble in water. Bile makes fat soluble by binding its fat-soluble end, exposing only its water-soluble end. Hence, the fat globule can be suspended in the water of the small intestine. The following diagram shows how bile works:

All fats have:

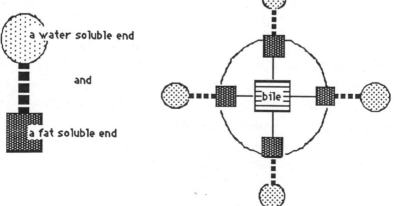

a water soluble end

and

a fat soluble end

Once dissolved the fat can be digested. In the following picture of fat breakdown, you will recognize some of the compounds from your acquaintance with heart and blood vessel disease.

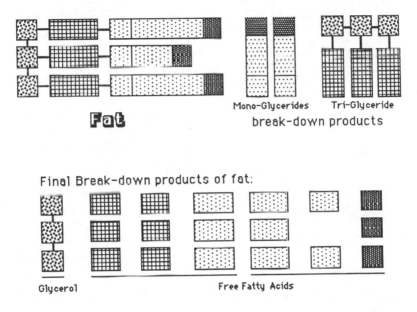

Fat

Mono-Glycerides   Tri-Glyceride

break-down products

Final Break-down products of fat:

Glycerol   Free Fatty Acids

Once these events have taken place, the final steps of intestinal digestion can occur. These happen at the level of the brush border, a layer of microscopic hairs which cover the small-intestinal cells like a beard (see diagram in next section). Refined activity occurs here which completes the digestion of these dietary particles. Brush border enzymes break proteins into amino acids, double sugars into simple sugars, fats into fatty acids, etc. Only then are they ready to be taken into the body through the walls of the intestine by absorption.

Absorption is accomplished through tiny pores in the lining cells of the intestine, and into the cells themselves. Fluid and some of the digested food particles are passively absorbed (much like water dripping through the pores of a coffee filter, taking with it the flavor of the coffee). Other particles are actively absorbed (individually moved across the lining cells, like carrying a pile of bricks, one at a time, from one point to another). The latter process requires energy for the act of absorption (in part explaining why some diets are slightly less fattening than others).

Thus, certain types of foods are absorbed *past* the lining cells and distributed throughout the body. These are usually changed into useful products in other locations in the body (liver, muscle, etc.), after delivery there by the blood stream. Others are absorbed *into* the lining cells. Some of these particles are further changed in the cells, making them useful to the body before being passed to the bloodstream. Many are used "as is."

Dietary proteins are broken into their component amino acids and fashioned into *human* proteins or are burned for calories. (Beef, fish, chicken and vegetable proteins don't simply *become* human protein. They are taken apart and rebuilt.) Proteins appear, for the most part, in enzymes and tissue, most notably bone and muscle. Fats are broken into simple fatty acids and carbon compounds. Except for energy there are few uses for fat. Sugars are used almost exclusively for calories. Thus, most of the food we eat is burned for calories.

Diet sustains the demands for energy in daily living. Only a fraction of the food is incorporated into our bodies as important tissue. When food is ingested in abundance it is stored as fat for future use. For all too many people in our society, excessive caloric intake is "banked" in well-recognized places, and stays there a long time since withdrawals are seldom made. Fortunately, fat in the bank doesn't draw interest!

STOMACH FACTORS

Food consumed is passed from the mouth, through the esophagus and into the stomach where the muscles mulch it into a puree. It is watered down by the stomach juices to a level consistent with the digestive processes which follow. Diluted food is passed into the small intestine in frequent small quantities. The time necessary for this process depends on a number of factors:

> Larger meals require larger amounts of water to dilute them and require more time for dilution to occur. This prolongs the emptying time of the stomach.

> Liquids consumed with meals ease the burden on the stomach to dilute the food, and shorten the time of emptying. Too much liquid with meals, however, can cause emptying of diluted foods unprepared for digestion.

> More water is necessary to dilute high-sugar meals, and they are more filling as well. Sugar draws water into the stomach, resulting in rapid dilution and over-filling. It also causes rapid emptying, or "dumping," after ulcer surgery.

Bulky, high-fiber meals are more "tenacious" and require more time for mulching before emptying.

Fat delays emptying of the stomach by producing internal hormonal effects. This allows time for fat to be emulsified by the bile, and further diluted to improve digestibility. High-fat meals thus dictate a longer time period before being emptied.

The physical structure and function of the stomach and intestine can be greatly changed by many factors. Foremost among these is surgery. For comparison, the normal stomach and intestine are shown in the illustration below.

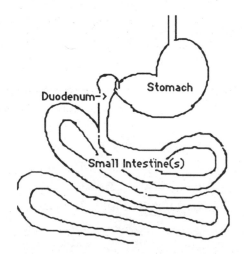

Normal Stomach and Intestine

Ulcer surgery usually results in cutting the stomach nerves and weakening, by-passing, or removing the outlet valve (pylorus). This removes normal controls and greatly hastens stomach emptying. In this situation, food often "dumps" into the small intestine. This is especially true for liquids and foods high in sugar. See illustration; shaded area represents part of intestine removed.

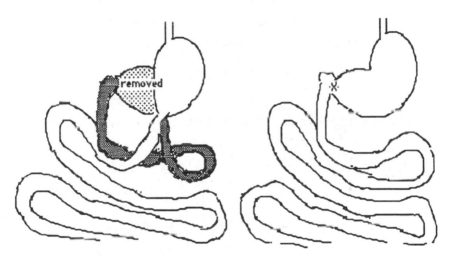

Ulcer Surgery By-Pass
This is also called Billroth Two.

Ulcer Surgery Pyloroplasty
x denotes widening of the pyloric opening. Billroth One is similar to this type.

Operations which by-pass much of the intestine, as formerly done for obesity, effectively shorten the intestine by exclusion of a portion of it. Further, they hasten emptying and transit time. These factors greatly affect digestion and absorption. See illustration on the following page; shaded area represents part of intestine by-passed.

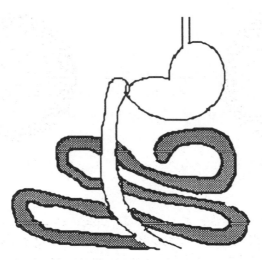

After Intestinal By-pass

Anything which hastens emptying of the stomach can affect lactose tolerance.

INTESTINAL CONSIDERATIONS

Between the stomach and the colon, within the brush border of the small intestine, lies the major site of trouble in the lactose-intolerant individual. It is here that lactase (the enzyme necessary to digest milk sugar) is supposed to be. When *lactase* is absent, or when its function is compromised, *lactose* is not digested, and the problem begins. The following section discusses the small intestine and what goes wrong.

The intestine is a very sophisticated muscular tube. Because of its folded lining, its villous projections and the "brush border," it has a surface area more than four times what it would be were it a simple, hollow tube. See illustration on the following page:

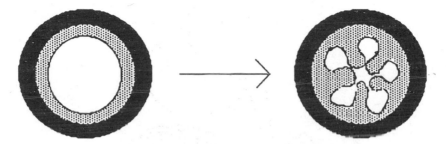

Demonstrates increase in lining by folding

The brush border is a very complex structure. It is a layer of tiny filaments: extensions of the lining cells of the small intestine. This border provides many enzymes, among them lactase, which finish the job of digestion immediately prior to absorption, making the brush border the active site of final digestion and absorption of many food products within the small intestine.

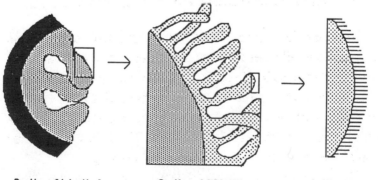

Section of intestinal
wall with fold

Section of fold with
villous projections

Section of villus
with brush border

Anatomy of a Villus

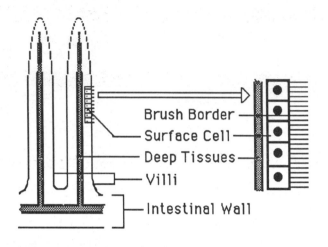

Brush Border
Surface Cell
Deep Tissues
Villi
Intestinal Wall

    The mixing action of the muscle produces turbulence--a constant rolling and tumbling--of the contents. Food thus contacts the intestinal wall repeatedly as it progresses through the digestive tract. Contact time necessary for absorption is a fraction of a second for most nutrients. When the intestine is overloaded with water, however, and therefore overstretched, food tends to flow inside the gut in a sheet-like fashion, as a jet-stream; see illustration on following page. When this jet stream propels food through this layer of turbulence, it is never exposed to the brush border. Things go rushing through without ever contacting the lining, in which case there is no opportunity for the final stages of digestion or absorption to take place. While this may result in the passage of recognizable food, more often it results in the passage of incompletely digested fats, proteins and starches.

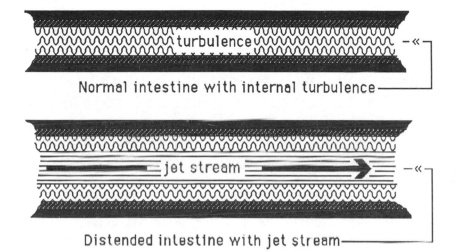

Normal intestine with internal turbulence

Distended intestine with jet stream

Intestinal movement is, then, closely associated with digestion and absorption and is influenced by many factors. In an overloaded gut (as occurs in lactose intolerance) and in the dumping syndrome (which occurs after ulcer surgery) there is little or no contact, as described above. There can be little wonder that nutrients are wasted in these situations.

Surgical removal (resection) of small intestine is sometimes done for inflammatory bowel diseases (Crohn's disease among them), for clotted blood vessels and for cancer. In other situations bowel is excluded, as in "the by-pass" for obesity. In these situations there is *no* exposure of the nutrients to the intestine; the ability to digest everything is altered. When large portions of the intestine are removed or excluded, lactose intolerance is often one of the lesser difficulties.

Because of complicating nerve diseases, the intestine often malfunctions in persons who have been diabetic for years, and in those with other nerve diseases such as multiple sclerosis. These situations are often complicated by poor stomach tone and even poorer emptying.

Problems such as overactivity of the thyroid, or taking too much thyroid medication, produce excessive activity of the intestine. Other hormonal imbalances can do similar things. Opposite possibilities also exist. Many metabolic illnesses are manifest by diarrhea or constipation due to their effects on intestinal activity.

Anxiety can influence intestinal activity. Almost everyone has experienced diarrhea or some intestinal symptom when under stress.

Many food products cause stimulation, irritation or relaxation. Certain drugs hasten intestinal movement and transit; others slow them down:

> Foods derived from the group which includes coffee, carob, and cocoa, often produce stimulation. They increase either stomach emptying or intestinal activity which often causes cramps or diarrhea. "Drugs" such as caffeine and mint can do the same.

> Fats can influence muscle tone of the valves or muscles of the intestine, influencing emptying time and intestinal activity.

> Prescription medicines such as Bentyl®, Combid®, Donnatal®, Levsin®, Lomotil®, Imodium®, codeine and the narcotic group all tend to slow intestinal activity. They generally reduce secretion

as well.

Other prescription drugs such as Reglan®, Urecholine® and thyroid medication tend to increase activity of the intestinal muscle.

Still others have intestinal effects: anti-depressants, tranquillizers and anti-hypertensive medications among them.

Consult your physician if symptoms persist despite your efforts; especially so if you are on any medications. Drugs can be a factor in the persistence of problems.

SUGAR, STARCH, AND LACTOSE

Since the subject of this book is lactose, a specific section on the digestion of sugar is appropriate. In nature most sugar occurs in the form of starch or cellulose, in which hundreds of single sugars are bound into large and complex forms. These substances represent the bulk of most food products from cereal grains to vegetables, and all vegetation from spores to trees. In forms such as cellulose (the chief constituent of cell walls of plants), the bonds are resistant to destruction, are undigestible by man, and represent the "dietary fiber" everyone talks about.

Digestion is necessary to render starch usable by the body. However, were it not for heat, much of the starch in food would be of no value to man. Cooking thus begins the process of transformation through which most of the energy in

starch is made available. Heat cleaves many of the complex
bonds, leaving smaller starch forms which can be further
divided by enzymes called amylases, found in saliva and the
pancreatic juice. When the simpler starches are chemically
split, much of what is left is in the disaccharide form (double
sugars). The principal disaccharide occurring in starch is
maltose. Other dietary disaccharides, sucrose and lactose (table
sugar and milk sugar), occur most commonly in their coupled
form.

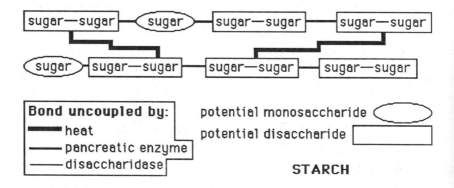

STARCH

Disaccharides are composed of monosaccharides or
single sugars; the most common of these simple dietary sugars
is glucose, most frequently referred to as blood sugar.
Splitting of these disaccharides is required in order for them to
be used. This is accomplished by enzymes called disaccharidases. There are three principal *disaccharides* in the
diet of man: lactose, maltose and sucrose. There are three
groups of specific *disaccharidases*, located in the brush border
of the intestine, which digest them: lactase, maltase and
sucrase. The disaccharides are brought into contact with the
brush border by intestinal muscular activity (peristalsis).

Instantaneously, they are split in two and absorbed through the lining cells.

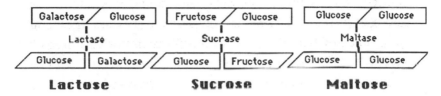

After final digestion, the simple sugars are absorbed through the intestinal lining in the same fashion as proteins and fats. Thereafter, sugar is used as energy for bodily function, or stored for future use. Stored sugar is in the form of glycogen (animal starch), and constitutes little more than three percent of the body weight. It is there as a ready source of quick energy. When abundant, glycogen is converted to fat for more permanent storage.

There are seven or eight varieties of disaccharidases which digest sucrose and a still larger number of these enzymes which digest maltose. There is, however, only one type of disaccharidase for lactose: *lactase*. In case of deficiency of these enzymes, which is common, the extra enzymes for sucrose and maltose serve as security systems. When it comes to lactose there is no backup available. When lactase is deficient, as it is in the majority of humans on our planet, there is no other way to handle the digestion of this sugar. The absence of this enzyme, or a back-up system, is likely the main reason that this particular digestive problem is so common.

EFFECTS OF LACTOSE MALDIGESTION

When lactose cannot be uncoupled, it cannot be absorbed, and is left within the intestine. Because it is thick and heavy it attracts water to dilute itself. When this happens, the fluid overload causes more muscle activity to clear the excess. Liquid and sugar go racing through the small intestine to the colon. The result is an awareness of this overactivity, and cramps are usually experienced by the afflicted individual.

The small intestine can absorb any fluid load delivered unless there is something wrong which prevents it from doing so. (Among the possible causes are diseases [infections], shortening [by-pass for obesity, or removal for cause], and lactose overload). The colon, by contrast, has a limited ability to absorb water. It is seldom normally exposed to more than a quart or two of liquid per day, and is not able to handle more than that.

Finally the water and sugar reach the colon. This organ is the end of the intestine where last-minute adjustments ordinarily take place. Here feces are given their final form, and here live most of the bacteria in the intestine. These organisms are accustomed to an environment loaded with food products undigestible by man. They are equipped to ferment the most resistant residue, as they must be in order to gain nutrients and energy for survival. When lactose reaches these bacteria they immediately attack, splitting it into hydrogen, water, organic acids and carbon dioxide. As a result the large intestine is full of organic acids, which it can absorb--gas and water, which it cannot. Absorption of the acids prevents important calorie wastage; malabsorption of carbon dioxide causes excessive gaseousness. When sufficient fluid overload occurs, diarrhea follows because the excess is not absorbed. Thus lactose produces symptoms, even misery, if ingested by those having little or no capability to digest it. This is especially so if large quantities of lactose are consumed.

Thus, the historic picture is complete: the afflicted individual ingests lactose, which cannot be digested or absorbed. As the water dilutes the sugar, the intestine becomes overdistended. There is overactivity--often cramping. The excessive activity results in the prompt arrival (often within minutes) of the sugar in the colon, and bacterial fermentation occurs, with gas and additional water its by-product. With large amounts of gas and liquid there is urgent diarrhea which can be vigorous and explosive. In cases of extreme overload, pressures within the colon can become so great as to overcome normal bowel reflexes, leading to incontinence. This is very embarrassing, and can be quite inconvenient even when it occurs in the privacy of the home. It does get one's attention, however, and will usually result in a visit for medical testing or opinion.

Unfortunately, even with this history, the diagnosis is commonly overlooked. Therefore, for emphasis:

1) Meal-related gaseousness should be presumed to be caused by lactose until proven otherwise.

2) Daily gaseousness, especially when progressive throughout the day, should be presumed to be caused by lactose until proven otherwise.

3) Chronic gaseousness, not otherwise explained, should be presumed to be caused by lactose until proven otherwise.

4) Lactose should be considered a related factor in resistant diarrhea until proven otherwise.

5) Gaseousness with diarrhea should be considered to be caused by lactose until proven otherwise.

6) Gaseousness or diarrhea persisting after "the flu" should be considered to be caused by lactose until proven otherwise.

7) Gaseousness or diarrhea occurring in a non-Caucasian should draw special attention regarding the possibility of lactose as a cause.

3

NUTRITIONAL GUIDELINES

Is it possible to be well-nourished on a lactose-restricted diet? Yes, if one plans his diet carefully to replace the nutrients that may be excluded when lactose-containing foods are omitted.

Milk is packed with vitamins, minerals, and protein, as well as with the culprit, lactose. If one simply stops drinking milk, chances are good there will be gaps in nutrient intake.

Ann, a 25-year-old woman, became aware of increasing gas and bloating, with occasional diarrhea. Her doctor diagnosed lactose intolerance. He told her to avoid milk and milk products. She did her best to eliminate milk from her diet and noticed a definite improvement in symptoms.

After several months, however, she began to have problems again. She was referred for nutritional counseling to determine if she was getting lactose in any form. A careful diet history showed that she had begun to use a new instant iced tea which contained lactose.

It was also apparent that her diet was not nutritionally adequate. She had eliminated milk completely, was using none of the allowable cheeses or milk substitutes, nor was she taking any vitamin/mineral supplements to replace the nutrients she was missing.

She was unaware that lactose-intolerant people often tolerate yogurt, buttermilk, and cottage cheese, or that Swiss, cheddar cheese, etc, are nearly lactose-free, so she avoided these foods, too. She rarely ate broccoli, spinach or other high calcium vegetables. Her diet was significantly low in calcium and riboflavin. This deficiency placed her at risk for osteoporosis, a loss of calcium from her bones, in later years.

After she became aware of the importance of correcting this situation, she began to include fortified milk substitutes, enzyme-treated milk, yogurt, cottage cheese and aged cheese in her diet on a regular basis.

Replacing the nutrients from milk with nutrients from other sources can help the diet to be nutritionally adequate, with or without vitamin and mineral supplements.

A healthy nutritious diet at all stages of life is important, whether or not an individual is lactose-intolerant. The selection of food for good nutrition requires planning, as well as knowledge of nutritional recommendations. First, let's consider guidelines for good nutrition in normal circumstances. It should be noted that the nutritional guidelines presented here are suited for adults and for children over the age of two years. Infant feeding is beyond the scope of *The Milk Sugar Dilemma.* Because of this, the Recommended Dietary Allowances for infants from birth to 12 months are not included in the discussion on nutrients. The limitations which lactose restriction places on the nutrition of younger children and infants can be harmful to their growth and development, unless it is competently planned and managed. If such limitations are necessary, medical and nutritional counseling are recommended.

The Basic Four Meal Plan is one of the handy guides for food selection to ensure an adequate diet. The Basic Four Meal Plan includes four groups of foods, *Milk, Meat & Protein, Fruits & Vegetables,* and *Grain.* The foods within each group supply similar nutrients and provide a variety of choices. Foods are chosen daily from each of the four groups.

The Milk Group contains foods providing the largest source of lactose. Therefore, many items in the Milk Group need to be significantly decreased, omitted, altered or substituted.

THE BASIC FOUR MEAL PLAN:

> *Milk Group*
>> 2 servings a day for adults
>> 3 servings for children
>> 4 servings for teens
>> 4 servings for pregnant and
>>> lactating women
>> Includes milk, yogurt, cottage
>>> cheese, cheese, and other
>>> milk products.

> *Meat and Protein Group*
>> 2 or more servings a day.
>> Includes meat, fish, poultry, eggs,
>>> dried beans and peas,
>>> lentils, legumes, and nuts.

> *Fruit and Vegetable Group*
>> 4 servings a day, including one
>>> serving high in Vitamin C
>>> and one high in Vitamin A.
>> Includes fresh or cooked fruits and
>>> vegetables, juices, berries, po-
>>> tatoes, etc.

Grain Group
>4 servings a day
>Includes whole-grain or enriched
>breads, pasta, cereal, rice, etc.

THE NUTRIENTS

When milk intake is reduced or omitted, the diet is likely to be deficient in the following nutrients:

>CALCIUM
>PROTEIN
>RIBOFLAVIN (VITAMIN B_2)
>VITAMIN A
>VITAMIN D

An overview of these nutrients will include the United States Recommended Dietary Allowances (U.S.RDA), nutrient standards set by the Food and Drug Administration, using the Recommended Dietary Allowances of the National Research Council. The U.S.RDAs are established for four age-sex groups. Generally, the highest values in the RDA table were selected for use within each U.S.RDA category. The nutritional information on food labels is expressed as percent of the U.S. RDA for adults. Dietary Allowances for specific age groups are located in SECTION 10.

CALCIUM

>U.S.RDA Requirement:
>>Children 1 to 4 years - 800 mg
>>Adult males and children 4+ yrs - 1000 mg
>>Adult women, pre-menopausal - 1200 mg
>>Adult women, post-menopausal - 1500 mg
>>Pregnant or lactating women - 1300 mg

Function: Although calcium is needed for building healthy teeth and bones in children, the body's need for this mineral is not confined to the growth years.

We know that the replacement of calcium in bones with calcium from the diet is an ongoing process. There will be a loss of calcium from the bones if there is inadequate calcium in the diet. The result of this process is called osteoporosis, a weakening of the bones. In older people, it is a major cause of fractures of the spinal column, the hip and the arm. To prevent osteoporosis, an adequate supply of calcium is necessary throughout life.

Osteoporosis becomes a more prevalent problem in women in their middle years. There are several factors which contribute to osteoporosis: decreased physical activity, hormonal changes occurring with menopause, and inadequate calcium intake in the diet, especially during pregnancy. Present recommendations for calcium intake for men is 1000 mg daily. The recommendations for women have been increased to 1200 mg-1500 mg in order to prevent loss of calcium from bones. During pregnancy and lactation, the recommended intake is 1300 mg.

Calcium performs other vital functions throughout life: contraction of muscles, excitation of nerves and clotting of blood.

Lactose-restricted sources: Calcium is found in enzyme-treated milk (Lactaid®, for example), calcium-fortified soy milk, and foods made with them, such as puddings, custard, and creamed dishes; dark green leafy vegetables; fish with small edible bones; natural aged cheese; cottage cheese, and yogurt; filberts and almonds.

Calcium is being added to a variety of foods previously not a source of calcium. The Pillsbury Company and General

Mills produce a flour which supplies 20% of the RDA per cup. Two biscuits made with the fortified flour contain 72 mg. of calcium. McDonald's is now manufacturing hamburger buns with added calcium for their fast-food chain. Citrus Hill Plus Calcium is a calcium-fortified orange or grapefruit juice beverage produced by Procter and Gamble. It supplies 300 mg. of calcium in an 8-ounce glass, an amount equivalent to milk.

Calcium content of a variety of foods is found in SECTION 10. Enzyme-treated milk and milk substitutes will be discussed in later sections.

Effects of inadequacy: A low intake of calcium causes osteoporosis (abnormal porosity of the bone), rickets, bone deformation, stunted growth, and abnormal sensation in the face.

PROTEIN

U.S.RDA Requirement:

Children 1 to 4 years - 28 gm

Adults and children 4 + years - 65 gm

Pregnant or lactating women - 95, 85 gm

Function: Protein provides amino acids, the building materials for growth, repair and maintenance of every cell; it regulates fluid balance between blood and cells. Protein is one of the energy-supplying nutrients, yielding 4 calories per gram.

Lactose-restricted sources: Protein is found in meat, poultry, fish, dried beans and peas, lentils, eggs, natural aged cheese, enzyme-treated milk, legumes, nuts, seeds and milk substitutes such as Vitamite®, Soyamel®, Isomil®, Ensure®, and Sustacal®. Yogurt, buttermilk, cottage cheese and ricotta cheese are protein foods which are tolerated by many lactose-intolerant persons. Two additional ounces of meat, fish, poultry, or cheese will replace the protein in 2 cups of milk.

Protein content of foods is found in SECTION 10. Enzyme-treated milk and milk substitutes will be discussed in later sections.

Effects of inadequacy: A low protein intake may cause loss of weight and muscle, decreased immune response, increased susceptibility to infection, and edema (swelling).

RIBOFLAVIN (VITAMIN B₂)

U.S.RDA Requirement:

Children 1 to 4 years - .8 mg

Adults and children 4 + years - 1.7 mg

Pregnant or lactating women - 2.0 mg

Function: Riboflavin assists in the release of energy from food in the body; it is a component in protein, carbohydrate, and fat metabolism.

Lactose-restricted sources: Riboflavin is found in enzyme-treated milk and foods made with it, such as pudding, custard, and creamed dishes; liver, and dark green leafy vegetables, whole grain breads and cereals; enriched grain products. Riboflavin content of foods is found in SECTION 10.

Effects of inadequacy: A low intake of riboflavin causes cheilosis (cracks at corners of the mouth), soreness of lips, redness of tongue, poor growth, increased prominence of blood vessels in the eye.

VITAMIN A

U.S.RDA Requirement:

Children 1 to 4 years - 2500 IU

Adults and children 4 + years - 5000 IU

Pregnant or lactating women - 8000 IU

Function: Vitamin A is an important component in the

visual process of the eye, including adaptation to dark; it assists in formation and maintenance of skin, mucous membranes, bones and teeth.

Lactose-restricted sources: Vitamin A is found in liver, carrots, sweet potatoes, dark green leafy vegetables, broccoli, winter squash, apricots, cantaloupe, peaches, enzyme-treated milk, fish liver oil. Vitamin A content of foods is found in SECTION 10.

Effects of inadequacy; A low intake of Vitamin A may cause xerophthalmia (an eye condition leading to night blindness), night blindness, permanent blindness and poor growth.

VITAMIN D
U.S.RDA Requirement:
> Children 1 to 4 years - 400 IU
> Adults and children 4 + years - 400 IU
> Pregnant or lactating women - 400 IU

Function: Vitamin D promotes mineralization of bones and teeth. It is necessary in the absorption and regulation of calcium and phosphorus in the body.

Lactose-restricted sources: Vitamin D is found in saltwater fish and their oils; fortified enzyme-treated milk, and lactose-free margarine, eggs, liver, and butter. It can be synthesized with skin exposure to sunlight. Ten minutes of sunlight daily on a large patch of skin provides adequate Vitamin D. Vitamin D content of foods is found in SECTION 10.

Effects of inadequacy: A low intake of Vitamin D may cause rickets (bone deformation) and softening of the bones (osteoporosis).

REPLACING THE NUTRIENTS OF MILK

If milk is omitted from the diet, it is important to plan substitutes carefully. The following figures will show specifically which nutrients need replacing.

Two cups of milk (the adult requirement) supply:

> 600 mg Calcium
> 16 gm Protein
> .8 mg Vitamin B_2 (Riboflavin)
> 600 International Units Vitamin A
> 200 International Units Vitamin D

These nutrients are needed daily. Occasionally eating of a piece of cheese, or now and then having a serving of dark green leafy vegetables is not sufficient to replace the missing nutrients. They must be obtained every day. To replace the nutrients in 2 cups of milk, one may substitute:

3 ounces (3 slices) of aged cheese (add bean sprouts and whole grain bread to the diet to increase riboflavin)

> or

2 cups of yogurt

> or

2 cups of pudding made with enzyme-treated milk or Soyamel®.

> or

2-1/2 cups of Soyamel® or 5 cups of Soyagen®; both are soy milk substitutes, but each is fortified with differing amounts of nutrients.

> or

4 cups of Vitamite®, a substitute for milk. Vitamin B_2 (Riboflavin) is not added to Vitamite®, therefore it is

necessary to incorporate adequate sources of riboflavin.

or

a combination of meat and vegetables, such as: 2 cups turnip greens + 1-1/2 ounces meat + 10 small mushrooms.

In addition, Vitamin D is necessary, either as a supplement or by exposure to sunlight. See the LACTOSE-RESTRICTED MENU PLANNER later in this section.

NUTRITIONAL ALTERNATIVES

It is possible to obtain the aforementioned vitamins and minerals from lactose-free sources. Protein is easily obtainable from meat. Vitamin A is readily obtained from fruits and vegetables, and Vitamin D can be converted in the skin by sunshine, but careful selection is required to obtain adequate calcium and riboflavin.

If the Milk Group is carefully examined, one will find there are several foods which can be chosen by lactose-intolerant individuals in order to assure an adequate intake of these essential nutrients. These sources include enzyme-treated milk, calcium-fortified soy milks, fermented dairy products, natural aged cheeses, and foods made with enzyme-treated milk or soy milk.

The most nutritionally efficient way to replace the nutrients in milk is to use **enzyme-treated milk**, which will contain all the vitamins and minerals found in regular milk. The amount needed daily would coincide with recommended amounts of regular milk. Enzyme-treated milk is discussed in greater detail in SECTION 6.

Cheese, cottage cheese, and ricotta cheese are

made from milk. In the process, milk is treated to allow the curd to be separated and removed from the whey. The solid curd is the protein portion of milk. The whey is the liquid portion. Since lactose dissolves in water, the whey takes with it most of the lactose, leaving cheese quite low in lactose. In the case of aged cheese, the aging process further reduces the lactose content, converting it to an easily digested by-product.

Yogurt and buttermilk are fermented dairy products. They seem to be much better tolerated than milk by lactose-intolerant individuals. The lactose content of yogurt and buttermilk are similar to lactose content of regular milk, but fail to produce symptoms in many lactose-intolerant people. The organisms and enzymes responsible for the fermentation of yogurt remain active in the finished product. These products contain lactase, the enzyme which digests milk sugar. As the yogurt is eaten by a lactose-intolerant individual and raised to body temperature, the lactase in the yogurt is digesting the milk sugar while it passes through the human digestive tract. This permits greater absorption of lactose by the lactose-intolerant individual than would otherwise be expected. The interested reader is referred to Lactose Intolerance and Yogurt, by Levitt and Savaiano, in *Practical Gastroenterology,* Jan./Feb., and Mar./Apr., 1985, Volume 9, No. 1 and 2.

Sweet acidophilus milk is another alternative. Developed at the University of North Carolina School of Dairy Science, it is a pasteurized skim or lowfat milk with a bacterial culture (Lactobacillus acidophilus) added. The bacteria remain inactive as long as the milk stays under 75°F. It is cooled immediately after the culture is added, so fermentation is prevented. The natural flavor and consistency of milk remain unchanged.

Once the sweet acidophilus milk is consumed, the

bacteria become active at body temperature. They break down lactose into lactic acid which can be easily absorbed by lactose-intolerant people. Similar to the yogurt theory, the bacteria in sweet acidophilus milk also may help to digest any remaining milk sugar as it passes through the small intestine. Sweet acidophilus milk, however, cannot be used in cooking or added to hot beverages because heat destroys the bacteria.

A word of caution: Imitation milk products are on the market which claim to be suitable for lactose-intolerant individuals. These products are *not* lactose-free. They contain nonfat dairy whey and nonfat dry milk powder. The lactose content is similar to that of powdered milk. They contain less than half the protein and calcium of milk, and more sugar in the form of corn syrup solids; therefore they are *not* nutritionally acceptable as milk substitutes.

TIPS ON TOLERATING MILK

Ingestion of small frequent amounts of lactose at one time is better tolerated. Try small amounts of milk several times a day instead of one large glass. Limit the amount of dairy foods at the same meal.

Milk with other foods reduces the concentration of lactose by slowing the stomach's emptying time. For example, try milk at regular meals or at snacktimes with cereal, in place of water in hot cereal, soups, macaroni, or rice, breads, or muffins.

Foods tolerated by some lactose-intolerant people are not well tolerated by others. It has been observed that chocolate milk and/or ice cream are better tolerated than whole milk; whole milk may be better tolerated than skim milk. The reason for this phenomenon may be dilution of sugars in the stomach or the effects of increased fat in delaying emptying of the stomach and the rate at which the stomach releases the milk sugar.

For example, chocolate milk and ice cream are higher in sugar than regular milk. Therefore, they call for more dilution of liquid from the stomach lining before they are allowed to leave the stomach. This dilutes the lactose as well. Chocolate milk and ice cream are higher in fat than whole milk or skim milk, thus delaying the emptying rate of the stomach. These foods may slow the rate of lactose through the small intestine enough to allow for more complete absorption. The higher fat content of whole milk may also explain why it is better tolerated by some individuals than skim milk. A trial of these foods will quickly let the individual know if he can tolerate them. If gas, bloating, and/or diarrhea occur, it is best to leave these foods alone.

VITAMIN AND MINERAL PILLS

Vitamin and mineral supplementation is a concern whenever a major group of foods is deleted from the diet. Careful food choices, as outlined in the preceding pages, can replace the nutrients adequately. Calcium is the most difficult nutrient to replace; therefore, calcium supplementation may be necessary. Adequate calcium is not usually found in a vitamin and mineral supplement; it may be obtained from calcium tablets, preferably in combination with Vitamin D.

Calcium tablets are available in several forms: calcium gluconate, calcium lactate, and calcium carbonate. These may vary in terms of cost and absorption rate, but are all effective supplements. Calcium from bone meal and dolomite should be avoided because of possible contamination from toxic metals.

The dose of calcium should not exceed recommended levels, because of the risk of urinary tract stones in some individuals. The tablets should provide 800-1000 mg calcium for adult males, 1200-1500 mg for women. Children, 1-10 years, require 800 mg, adolescent boys and girls require 1200 mg. Pregnant and nursing mothers require an additional 400 mg. See Recommended Dietary Allowances (RDA) in SECTION 10.

If further vitamin/mineral supplementation is deemed necessary by the physician or dietitian, a supplement may be used which supplies no more than 100% of the Recommended Dietary Allowances. The vitamins to include are Vitamin A, Vitamin D, and riboflavin. Amounts vary for small children, teens, pregnant and nursing mothers. The reader is again referred to the RDA in SECTION 10.

Vitamin/mineral supplements should be taken only in recommended amounts. Overdoses can occur when these products are misused. An excessive intake of calcium can cause urinary tract stones and heart irregularities. An overdose of Vitamin A can cause yellow pigmentation of skin, loss of appetite, and vomiting. An overdose of Vitamin D can lead to poor growth, weight loss, vomiting, poor appetite, and calcium deposition in soft tissues.

LACTASE PILLS

Lactase pills are available which have been shown to reduce symptoms associated with lactose intake in some people. The pills contain lactase, the enzyme required for lactose digestion. A protective coating on the pills permits the intact enzyme to reach the small intestine where it promotes lactose absorption. The pills are most effective when they are taken just prior to the intake of lactose-containing meals.

Lactase pills may be effective in reducing symptoms for many people, especially if taken prior to meals away from home when lactose content is unknown. These products may not work as effectively as lactose avoidance for those individuals with hypermotile gastrointestinal tracts, because of the extremely rapid passage of lactose and lactase through the small intestine past the sites of absorption. The timing of the dissolving of the protective coating of the lactase pill is critical. The coating must be intact in the stomach so the lactase enzyme won't be digested, and therefore become ineffective. Then the coating must quickly dissolve before the enzyme rushes through the small intestine along with the milk sugar.

Lactase pills are available at pharmacies and some specialty food stores. Included among them are Lactrase®, a capsule made by Kremers-Urban Company of Milwaukee, Wisconsin 53201, and Lactaid® Tablets, by Lactaid, Inc., P.O. Box 111, Pleasantville, NJ 08232. A newcomer to the market is Dairy-Gest, made by Dairy-Gest Farms, Inc., 2666 Winona Road, Baldwin, New York 11510, telephone (212) 279-5635. It is reputed to be half the price and four times the potence of the others, making it much less costly to use-- probably with enhanced effectiveness.

LACTOSE-RESTRICTED MENU PLANNER

The LACTOSE-RESTRICTED MENU PLANNER provides a guide for meal planning to allow for a wide selection of foods within lactose-restricted limitations. Often the frustrated patient says, "I *know* what I need to avoid, but what can I *have*?" By making selections within these lists, the meal plans will be lactose-restricted and nutritious.

The choices within each group which supply a significant amount of Vitamin A, Vitamin B_2, or Vitamin C, are indicated. Foods of significant calcium content are noted, also. Calcium content of the Milk Choices are compared to 8 ounces of milk. Ensure®, Ensure Plus®, Isocal®, Sustacal® contain less calcium than an equal amount of milk because these products are designed to avoid exceeding the RDA for calcium in quantities up to 6 cups when given as nutritional formulae.

It should be emphasized that all foods on these lists contribute to the total daily intake of nutrients, with the exception of many of the Extra Choices, which supply only calories. Selection of a variety of foods is important in planning a nutritious diet.

SAMPLE MENUS illustrate the use of these lists, and are located at the conclusion of the LACTOSE-RESTRICTED MENU PLANNER.

Nutrient data from which the MENU PLANNER was derived are listed in the TABLE OF SELECTED NUTRIENT CONTENT OF VARIOUS FOODS in SECTION 10. Nutrients include calories, protein, Vitamin A, Vitamin D, riboflavin, and calcium.

MILK CHOICES   One cup (8 ounces) equals one serving

       2 servings a day for adults

       3 servings for children

       4 servings for teens

       4 servings for pregnant and lactating women

*Buttermilk Vitamin B2, Calcium

  Cheese, natural aged Vitamin A, Calcium

*Cottage Cheese Vitamin A, Vitamin B2

Ensure® Vitamin A, Vitamin B2, 1/2 Calcium

Ensure Plus® Vitamin A, Vitamin B2, 1/2 Calcium

Isocal® Vitamin A, Vitamin B2, 1/2 Calcium

Isomil® Vitamin A, Vitamin B2, Calcium

Lactaid® in milk Vitamin A, Vitamin B2, Calcium

Soyamel® Vitamin A, Vitamin B2, Calcium

Sustacal® Vitamin A, Vitamin B2, Calcium

Vitamite® Vitamin A, 1/2 Calcium - contains no riboflavin (B2).

*Yogurt Vitamin A, Vitamin B2, Calcium

*These lactose-containing products may be tolerated. These should not be used in initial stages of lactose-restricted diet, but may be tried later.

MEAT AND PROTEIN CHOICES

> 2 3-oz. servings a day
>
> 3 3-oz. servings for pregnant women

Beef Vitamin B

Lamb Vitamin B2

Pork Vitamin B2

Veal Vitamin B2

Liver Vitamin A, Vitamin B2

Poultry Vitamin B2

Fish Vitamin A, (Calcium if bones are edible)

Egg Vitamin A, Vitamin B2

Cold Cuts--read labels

Frankfurters--read labels

Nuts and seeds

> Almonds
>
> Filberts
>
> Peanuts, roasted
>
> Sesame Seeds Calcium
>
> Sunflower Seeds Vitamin B2, Calcium

Peanut Butter

FRUIT AND VEGETABLE CHOICES

Select 4 servings per day. Be sure one is high in Vitamin C and one is high in Vitamin A. If a limited amount of milk or milk products is selected, be sure one is high in riboflavin (B_2).

FRUIT	**VEGETABLES**
Apple	Asparagus Vit A, Vitamin B2
Apple juice	Avocado Vitamin A, Vitamin B2
Applesauce	Baked beans Vitamin A, Calcium
Apricots Vitamin A	Bean sprouts Vitamin B2
Banana Vitamin B2	Beets
Blueberries	Broccoli Vitamin A, Vitamin B2, Vitamin C
Cantaloupe Vitamin C	Brussels sprouts VitB2 & C
Cherries	Cabbage Vitamin A, Vitamin C
Cranberries	Carrots Vitamin A
Dates	Cauliflower Vitamin C
Figs	Celery
Grapefruit, pink Vit A & C	Cucumbers
Grapefruit juice Vitamin C	Eggplant
Grapes	Green beans Vitamin A
Grape juice	Green peppers Vitamin A
Honeydew	Lima beans Vitamin A
Kiwi fruit Vitamin A & C	Mushrooms Vitamin B2
Lemon Vitamin C	Okra Vitamin A, Vitamin B2
Limes Vitamin C	Onions
Mango Vitamin A, Vitamin C	Peas Vitamin A, Vitamin B2
Nectarine Vitamin A & B2	Potatoes
Orange Vitamin A, Vitamin C	Pumpkin Vitamin A
Orange juice Vitamin A & C	Rhubarb Vitamin A, Calcium
Papaya Vit A, Vitamin B2 & C	Rutabaga Vitamin A
Peach Vitamin A	Snow peas
Pear	Spinach Vitamin A & B2
Pineapple	Summer squash Vitamin A

Pineapple juice

Plums Vitamin A

Prunes Vitamin A, Vitamin B2

Prune juice Vitamin B2

Raisins Vitamin B2

Strawberries Vitamin B2 & C

Tangarine Vitamin A, Vitamin C

Watermelon Vitamin A

Tomatoes Vitamin A & C

Turnip greens Vit A, B2, Calcium

Wax beans Vitamin A

Winter squash Vit A & B2

Yams Vitamin A

Zucchini Vitamin A

GRAIN CHOICES

Select 4 choices per day.   If less than two servings from the milk group are selected, emphasize foods high in riboflavin (Vitamin B$_2$).

Bread

Bagel Vitamin B2

Cracked wheat bread Vitamin B2 - check labels

English muffins Vitamin B2 - check labels

French bread

Italian bread

Rolls, buns Vitamin B2 - check labels

Rye bread, pumpernickel Vitamin B2

Tortilla Vitamin B2

Vienna bread

White bread

Cereal

Cereal, ready to eat, fortified Vitamin A, B2, & C

Cereal, cooked

Rice or barley Vitamin B2

Pasta Vitamin B2

Wheat germ Vitamin B2

Crackers
> Graham crackers - check labels
> Pretzels
> Saltines, Zesta®, or Ritz®, or check labels

Flours
> White flour Vitamin B2
> Cornstarch
> Cornmeal Vitamin A, Vitamin B2

EXTRA CHOICES
> Select from this group to supplement calories.

Fats
> Bacon
> Butter Vitamin A
> Coffeemate®
> Coffee Rich®
> French dressing
> Italian dressing
> Margarine Vitamin A - check label
> Mayonnaise
> Nuts, if tolerated
> Vegetable oil

Miscellaneous
> Broth, bouillon
> Catsup Vitamin A
> Coffee and tea, if tolerated
> Hard sugar candy - check label
> Herbs, spices (Chili powder, red pepper,
>> cayenne pepper, paprika, oregano and parsley are
>> high in Vit. A in commonly used amounts)
> Pickles Vitamin A
> Vinegar

Desserts and Sweets
  Angelfood cake
  Fruit pie
  Fruit ice - check label
  Gelatin
  Jams, jellies

SAMPLE MENUS

The SAMPLE MENUS illustrate the use of the MENU PLANNER. Starred items (*) indicate recipes to be found in SECTION 8. The symbol (#) indicates packaged foods, some brands of which contain lactose. Brand names are elaborated upon in SECTION 9.

For each menu, be sure to include 2 servings from the Milk Choices; for example, 2 cups Soyamel®, 4 cups Vitamite®, etc. Some of the Milk Choices may be used in cooking to increase intake. If tolerance to enzyme-treated milk, yogurt and cottage cheese has been demonstrated, these are good choices from the Milk Group.

Breakfast	Lunch	Dinner
Day 1		
Orange Juice	Ham Sandwich#	Meat Loaf*
Poached or	Bibb Lettuce with	Mashed Potatoes*
Soft Cooked Egg	Tomato Slices	Steamed Broccoli
Toast# with	Sliced Peaches	Roll# and
Margarine#		Margarine#
		Garden Salad /
		Fr.Dressing
		Fruit Cup

Day 2

Grapefruit Half	Chef Salad with	Baked Chicken
Dry Cereal# with	Aged Cheddar,	Rice
Vitamite	Sliced Turkey,	Turnip Greens
Toast#	and Sliced egg	Mandarin Salad
with Margarine#	Muffin#*	Bread# with
		Margarine#
		Angelfood Cake

Day 3

Apple Juice	Hamburger Patty on	Broiled Fish
Poached Egg	Bun# with	Boiled Potatoes
Biscuits#*	Tomato Slices	Asparagus
with Margarine#	Dill Pickles	Lettuce Salad/
	and Mayonnaise	Fr. Dressing
	Fresh Apple	Roll# with
		Margarine#
		Cherry Pie

Day 4

Banana	Turkey and	Roast Beef with
Oatmeal with	Swiss Cheese	Mushrooms
Vitamite	Sandwich#	Mashed Potato#
Toast#	Orange Sections	Spinach
with Margarine#		Bread# with
		Margarine#
		Fresh Fruit

Day 5

Frozen Orange Juice	Chicken Salad	Sliced Ham
Omelette*	on Lettuce	Baked Beans
Dry Cereal# with	Fresh Vegetables	Carrots/Peas
Vitamite	Crackers#	Roll#
Toast#	Apricots	Coleslaw
with Margarine#		Applesauce

VEGETARIAN DIETS WITH
LACTOSE RESTRICTION

A lactose restriction on a vegetarian diet can be a significant nutritional problem, unless it is undertaken with a consideration for the nutrients which may be lacking.

There are several types of vegetarian diets; the two most popular are the vegan diet and the lacto-ovo vegetarian diet. The vegan diet or "strict" vegetarian diet consists only of foods of plant origin, i.e. fruits, vegetables, grains, legumes, nuts, and seeds. The lacto-ovo vegetarian diet includes foods of plant origin in addition to milk, milk products, and eggs.

A vegetarian diet has the potential for deficiencies of various nutrients unless *carefully* planned. These nutrients include protein, iron, zinc, calcium, riboflavin (Vitamin B_2), Vitamin B_{12}, and Vitamin D. Unless enzyme-treated milk or fortified soy milk is used, the intake of the lactose-intolerant vegetarian is likely to be low in several of these nutrients. Each nutrient will be discussed and recommendations given for assuring an adequate intake.

PROTEIN: For growth, maintenance, and repair of body tissue, humans require the nine essential amino acids in their diets. Dietary proteins that contribute all of the essential amino acids in the amounts needed are referred to as complete proteins, or proteins of high biological value. In the vegetarian diet, complete proteins are found in eggs, milk, milk products, and for some vegetarians, fish and poultry. Lactose-intolerant lacto-ovo vegetarians can use eggs, natural aged cheese, and enzyme-treated milk for their sources of complete proteins. Most lactose-intolerant vegetarians can tolerate limited quantities of cottage cheese, ricotta cheese, yogurt and buttermilk.

All plant proteins, except soy, contain less than the required amount of at least one essential amino acid. The essential amino acid that is present in the least amount is called the limiting amino acid. Therefore, the amount of protein to be built in the body from amino acid "building blocks" will be limited by the amino acid present in the least amount.

Grains tend to be low in lysine and high in methionine. Legumes, with the exception of peanuts, are low in methionine and tryptophan and high in lysine. Nuts and seeds are primarily deficient in lysine. To obtain the required amount of each of the essential amino acids in a vegetarian diet, a combination of foods of plant origin should be used. For example, Boston baked beans may be the main course in a meal. Although the protein quantity may be adequate, the protein quality is not, because beans are low in methionine. To improve the protein quality and "build" a complete protein, a protein source high in methionine, such as whole wheat bread, should be added to the meal. Thus, the foods are complements. Hence, we have Boston Baked Beans and Brown Bread as a traditional and nutritious combination.

Other foods which have complementary amino acids are shown in the table below:

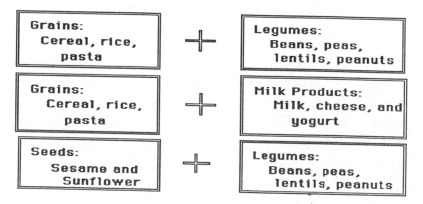

Grains: Cereal, rice, pasta	+	Legumes: Beans, peas, lentils, peanuts
Grains: Cereal, rice, pasta	+	Milk Products: Milk, cheese, and yogurt
Seeds: Sesame and Sunflower	+	Legumes: Beans, peas, lentils, peanuts

Vegans, vegetarians who do not consume eggs or milk, must select complementary proteins because most of their supply of essential amino acids depends on combining foods of plant origin. It is recommended that vegans consume 2-3 servings of soy milk and/or tofu, or soy curd. Soy milk contains 5-6 grams of protein per cup; tofu contains 12 grams of protein per cup. These products are complete proteins, and may be eaten singly or in combination with incomplete protein foods.

IRON AND ZINC: These two minerals are of concern for all vegetarians, lactose-intolerant or not, since milk is not a prime source of either iron or zinc. Vegetarians can obtain iron in legumes, whole or enriched grains, greens, nuts, and certain fruits. Iron absorption is enhanced by including a source of Vitamin C, such as citrus fruit, strawberries, tomatoes or broccoli with iron-containing foods. Zinc in the vegetarian diet is found in legumes, whole grains, and nuts.

CALCIUM: The richest, most reliable and practical sources of dietary calcium are milk, milk products, and calcium-fortified soy milk. Lactose-intolerant persons following a lacto-ovo vegetarian diet should easily meet their calcium needs with enzyme-treated milk, when tolerated, or with soy milks, in addition to milk products such as natural aged cheese. Most individuals tolerate cottage and ricotta cheese, yogurt, and buttermilk. Calcium intake can also be increased by eating broccoli, turnip greens, almonds and filberts, seeds, legumes, tofu, and fish with small edible bones.

Vegans, in contrast, may have difficulty obtaining calcium in adequate amounts (1000 mg) unless careful food selections are made. A vegan is advised to consume calcium-fortified soy milks. Or he could consume 1-1/4 cups of cooked turnip greens or 2 cups of cooked broccoli to obtain as much

calcium as 1 cup of milk (291 mg.). The following chart
shows calcium content of foods from plant sources. However,
part of the calcium is tied up with other minerals in many of the
dark green leafy vegetables on this list, and some of the
calcium is not able to be absorbed into the body.

CALCIUM CONTENT OF FOODS

FOOD	SERVING SIZE	CALCIUM MG
VEGETABLES, COOKED		
BROCCOLI	1 CUP	117
COLLARDS	1 CUP	304
DANDELION GREENS	1 CUP	280
KALE	1 CUP	233
MUSTARD GREENS	1 CUP	276
TURNIP GREENS	1 CUP	244
LEGUMES, COOKED		
LIMA BEANS	1 CUP	64
NAVY BEANS	1 CUP	95
BLACKEYED PEAS	1 CUP	43
GREAT NORTHERN BEANS	1 CUP	90
PINTO BEANS	1 CUP	270
NUTS AND SEEDS		
ALMONDS	1/2 CUP	240
FILBERTS	1/2 CUP	146
SESAME	1/2 CUP	83
SUNFLOWER	1/2 CUP	87
SOY MILK	1 CUP	240
TOFU	1 CUP	260
MOLASSES, BLACKSTRAP	1 TABLESPOON	116

VITAMIN D: This nutrient is not found in foods of plant
origin. As previously mentioned, Vitamin D is synthesized in
the body as a result of exposing the skin to sunlight. If daily
sunlight exposure is minimal, it is important to obtain Vitamin
D from foods, such as Vitamite®, fortified soy milk
(Soyamel®), or fortified enzyme-treated milk. It is especially

important for children and pregnant and lactating women to obtain adequate amounts of Vitamin D.

VEGETARIAN MEAL PLANS

In planning menus for the lactose-intolerant vegetarian, it is important to use an appropriate meal plan or guide, such as those described in *Dietetic Currents*, January, 1983, Ross Laboratories, by Fanelli and Kuczmarski. This information is reprinted with permission of Ross Laboratories, Columbus, OH 43216.

The food guides, adapted here for the lactose-restricted diet, are designed to assure nutritionally adequate meal patterns. Foods which are of comparable nutritive value are grouped together. The major nutrients contributed by the food groups are listed below.

Note: The nutrients needed to replace those in milk are **in bold print.**

GROUP I
CEREALS AND WHOLE GRAINS - provide **protein, riboflavin (B$_2$),** fiber, iron, magnesium, zinc, niacin, pyridoxine (B$_6$), and thiamine. Standard Serving: 1 slice whole grain or enriched bread or 3/4 cup cooked cereal or 3/4 cup dry cereal.

GROUP II
LEGUMES AND MEAT ALTERNATIVES - provide **protein, calcium, phosphorus,** iron, magnesium, zinc, thiamine, niacin, and ascorbic acid if the legume is sprouted. Standard Serving: 1 cup cooked legume or 2 to 3 ounces soy

meat analog or 1 ounce textured vegetable protein.

NUTS AND SEEDS - provide **protein, calcium, phosphorus, riboflavin (B_2)**, iron, magnesium, zinc, niacin, and thiamine. Standard Serving: 3 Tablespoons.

GROUP III

MILK AND MILK PRODUCTS - provide **protein, calcium, phosphorus, Vitamin A, Vitamin D (if products are fortified), riboflavin (B_2)**, Vitamin B_6 and B_{12}. Lactose-restricted foods in the Milk Group include enzyme-treated milk, fortified soy milk, natural aged cheese, and for many lactose-intolerant individuals, yogurt, buttermilk, cottage cheese and ricotta cheese. Standard Serving: 1 cup enzyme-treated milk, 1 cup fortified soy milk, 2-inch cube of cheese, 1 cup yogurt, 1 cup cottage cheese, or 1 cup buttermilk.

EGGS - Egg white provides **protein and riboflavin (B_2)**, while egg yolk provides **protein, Vitamin A, riboflavin (B_2)**, cholesterol, Vitamin B_6, B_{12}, and thiamine. Standard Serving: 1 medium egg.

GROUP IV

FRUITS AND VEGETABLES - provide **calcium, Vitamin A, riboflavin (B_2)**, fiber, iron, magnesium, potassium, ascorbic acid, and folic acid. Standard Serving: 1/2 cup juice or 1 medium piece or 1 cup raw or 1/2 cup cooked.

GROUP V

FATS AND OILS - provide **Vitamins A, D,** and K. Standard Serving: 1 Tablespoon of any fat or oil.

Since differences exist in the nutrient content of specific foods within each group, it is important to select from a wide variety of foods in each group. By observing the **nutrients in bold print** one can see that the nutrients usually obtained from milk can be obtained from the vegetarian lactose-restricted diet plan. Details of the plan follow:

FOOD GUIDE FOR LACTOSE-RESTRICTED ADULT LACTO-OVO VEGETARIAN DIETS

FOOD GROUP		MINIMUM NUMBER OF SERVINGS DAILY	
		Males	Females
I	Cereals, whole grains, breads	8	6
II.	Legumes, meat analogs, textured vegetable proteins	1	3/4
	Nuts, seeds	1	1
III.	Milk, milk products	1-1/2	1-1/2
	Eggs	1-1/2	1-1/2
IV.	Fruits, vegetables	6	5
V.	Oils	1	1

From Fanelli, M. T., and Kuczmarski, R. J., Food Selection for Vegetarians, *Dietetic Currents*, January, 1983, Ross Laboratories. Reprinted with permission of Ross Laboratories, Columbus, OH 43216

Notes on the Lacto-Ovo-Vegetarian Diet:

The figures refer to number of servings per day. See the description of serving size in the discussion of nutrients provided in each group.

For a lacto-ovo-vegetarian diet for children and teens, it is advisable to consult a physician and/or dietitian for proper amounts from each group to meet the needs of growth and development.

Pregnant women should have at least six servings of whole grains and breads. They should have at least two servings of legumes and four servings of enzyme-treated milk or soy milk. Due to the increased requirements of pregnancy and lactation combined with the existing restrictions imposed by lactose intolerance, it is advisable to seek advice from a physician and/or dietitian to assure a nutritionally adequate diet during pregnancy and lactation.

FOOD GUIDE FOR ADULT VEGAN DIETS

Food Group	Minimum Number of Servings Daily*	Estimated protein per Serving
I. Bread, 1 slice	4	2 grams
Whole Grains, 1 cup	3-5	4 grams
II. Legumes, 1 cup	2	10 grams
Nuts or Seeds, 3 Tbsp.	1	5 grams
IV. Fruits, 1/2 cup	1-4	-
Vegetables,1/2 cup cooked		
or 1 cup raw	4	2 grams
V. Oils, 1 Tbsp.	1	-

Notes on the Vegan Diet:

*Serving Sizes - 1 slice whole grain or enriched bread; 1 cup cooked cereal or whole grains; 1 cup cooked legumes, 3 tablespoons nuts or seeds; 1/2 cup fruit juice; 1/2 cup cooked or 1 cup raw vegetables; and 1 tablespoon oil.

If the Vegan diet is used for children, fortified soy milk, such as Soyamel®, should be used to ensure adequate nutrition. Vitamin D and B_{12} supplements are recommended. It is advisable to seek advice from a physician and/or dietitian.

Pregnant women should add 4 cups of soy milk which has been fortified with calcium and Vitamin B_{12}. Iron and folic acid supplements are generally recommended during pregnancy.

As previously mentioned, due to the increased requirements of pregnancy and lactation combined with the existing restrictions imposed by lactose intolerance, it is advisable to seek advice from a physician and/or dietitian to assure a nutritionally adequate diet.

4

THE LACTOSE-
RESTRICTED DIET

The degree of lactose intolerance varies from one individual to another, depending on genetic tendencies, age, gastrointestinal susceptibility, etc. Guidelines for determining individual degree of lactose intolerance are described in SECTION 5. One individual may not tolerate lactose in any food, while another may be able to consume several servings of foods containing varying amounts of lactose, whey, milk solids, etc. When he exceeds a certain amount of lactose, he begins to have symptoms.

For example, Tom is one of those relatively rare individuals who cannot tolerate any lactose; if he consumes even one slice of bread made with milk solids, he experiences gas and bloating. In the second example, Mary has found she can tolerate six slices of bread made with milk solids, six teaspoons of margarine containing whey, in addition to a half cup of milk every day. If she exceeds this amount of lactose, however, she can count on having abdominal cramping, gas, bloating, and usually diarrhea.

In the first case, Tom must select his foods only from the ACCEPTABLE CHOICES and avoid all foods on the AVOID

OR USE SPARINGLY list. In the second case, Mary knows the amount of lactose-containing foods she can tolerate, selects most of her foods from the ACCEPTABLE CHOICES and cautiously selects items from the AVOID OR USE SPARINGLY lists. She might, for instance, select a roll with milk solids, and omit a slice of bread with milk solids, thus keeping her total lactose intake fairly constant. In this way, she avoids unwanted symptoms.

Since lactose occurs naturally only in milk, we can make certain assumptions about many types of foods which do not contain lactose. Fresh plain meats, poultry, fish, eggs, vegetables, fruits, and grains do not contain lactose. Milk, milk products and foods made with added milk, lactose, or whey, do contain lactose.

If we lived on a farm and grew all our own food, we could be assured that the only foods on our table which contained lactose would be the ones to which we added milk. If we could not tolerate lactose, we would not eat the puddings, cakes, breads, creamed dishes, etc., that had been made in our own kitchen.

However, most of us do not grow or prepare all of our own food. Most of what we eat has undergone some sort of preparation before it is purchased by us. Plain frozen or canned foods usually do not have any added lactose. It is during the commercial preparation of fresh foods that lactose may be added. The clue to understanding a lactose-restricted diet, then, is to think about which foods have undergone any preparation before we buy them, or which foods are likely to be made with milk.

Label reading is essential when planning a lactose-restricted diet. Some items which are ACCEPTABLE CHOICES include a statement that not all brands of that particular product will be lactose-free. The labels of various brands of such products must be checked to determine if lactose, whey, or milk is included. If whey, lactose, milk, or milk solids appear on the label, the product contains lactose and may need to be avoided.

Many food companies responded to requests for information on the lactose content of their products. Their listings of lactose-free foods are found in SECTION 9. Refer to these lists for specific brand names which are lactose-free; all companies advise consumers to check the actual label from time to time to determine if there has been a change in ingredients.

Most manufacturers provided data only on the foods which are lactose-free. They were, for the most part, unable to provide information on the quantity of lactose present in foods containing whey, lactose, or milk solids. This may be due to the variation of lactose content depending on which type of whey or milk substance is available to a manufacturer at a particular time. Some whey is lower in lactose than other types of whey. The type used depends on cost and availability.

If lactose content information becomes more available in the future, a food substitution system could be devised for lactose-intolerant people to accurately determine and plan their lactose intake. At the present time, such a method is impossible.

The following several pages contain the food lists of the LACTOSE-RESTRICTED DIET. They are arranged by categories in alphabetical order, as follows:

BEVERAGES	POTATOES & STARCHES
BREADS, ROLLS,	SEASONINGS
& CEREAL	SOUPS

DESSERTS & FRUITS   SWEETS & CANDIES
FATS, OILS, & NUTS   VEGETABLES
MEATS & SUBS   MISCELLANEOUS
plus AGING TIME OF CHEESE

BEVERAGES

ACCEPTABLE CHOICES:

Milk substitutes, including Vitamite®, and soy milk, such as Soyagen®, Soyamel®, Isomil®, Nursoy®, Prosobee®, Isocal®. Nutritional supplements such as Sustacal®, Ensure®, and Ensure Plus®.

Enzyme-treated milks, such as Lactaid® or Lacteeze: lactose content varies for each of these, depending on amount of enzyme added and length of treatment time; see directions on labels.

Buttermilk (not lactose-free, but likely to be tolerated).

Carbonated beverages and powdered fruit drinks without lactose.

Sugarfree drink mixes, such as Crystal Lite®. Read labels.

Fruit juices, vegetable juices. Fruit drinks, if lactose-free.

Coffee, decaffeinated coffee, cocoa powder, Nestle's Quik®, regular tea, instant iced tea if 100% pure tea.**

Most alcoholic beverages**.

Coffee substitutes including Postum®, Pero®, Caffex®, and decaffeinated teas.

Borden's Cremora®, Carnation Coffeemate®, Rich's Coffee Rich®*.

*The nondairy creamers are high in saturated fat. Their use should be limited or avoided by individuals who must restrict their intake of saturated fats or cholesterol.

**In certain medical situations, these beverages may be irritating or stimulating to the gastrointestinal tract. Check with your physician and/or dietitian.

AVOID OR USE SPARINGLY:
Whole milk, low fat, skim milk, or chocolate milk.

Powdered milk, sweetened condensed milk, evaporated milk, milk solids.

Cream, half and half, whipping cream.

Most instant chocolate beverages, Ovaltine®.

Most instant breakfast drinks; most weight reduction formulas.

Some instant iced tea beverages with added lactose to improve dissolving.

Milk chocolate.

Some powdered fruit drink mixes.

Some new imported carbonated beverages, example: Rivella®.

Some cordials and liqueurs, wine with sugar added. Lactose is usually not indicated on the label of cordials, liqueurs, and wines. Either avoid them or test your tolerance to them in small quantities.

BREADS, ROLLS, AND CEREAL

ACCEPTABLE CHOICES:
Breads made with water, such as Italian, Vienna, or French breads, Jewish rye bread, any Jewish bakery products, Hillbilly® bread by Schafer Bakery, most Schafer® breads. These breads usually have a hard crisp crust.

Premium® Saltines, Zesta® Saltines, Ry-Krisp® and Ritz® crackers, rusk, graham crackers, and other crackers without lactose, whey, or milk.

General Mills Bows®, Bugles®; other snack chips without lactose.

Baked products prepared at home which are made without milk.

Most dry cereals. Cooked or dry cereals without added milk. A milk substitute may be used on cereals. Fruit juices may be used on cereals for variety. Infant cereals without lactose or milk solids.

AVOID OR USE SPARINGLY:

Breads and rolls to which milk, lactose, or whey is added. These breads usually have a soft crust.

Biscuits, muffins, pancakes, sweet rolls, doughnuts, waffles, unless made without milk.

Most hamburger and hot dog buns.

Bread and roll mixes, refrigerator rolls, unless made without milk, lactose, or whey.

Dry cereals containing lactose, whey, or milk solids, such as Special K® and Cocoa Krispies®, General Mills Crackers Cereal®, Post Fortified Oat Flakes®, C. W. Post Hearty Cereals®. Cereals cooked with milk. Some instant cereals.

DESSERTS AND FRUIT

ACCEPTABLE CHOICES:

Any dessert made without milk products, such as angelfood cake, gelatin desserts, milk-free cookies and cakes, most fruit pies, pie crust.

Chocolate desserts made without milk, using cocoa powder or Hershey's semi-sweet chocolate.

Water ices, fruit ices, most Italian ices, most sorbets.

Popsicles; fruit juice bars, such as Minute Maid Juicees.

Many pudding mixes and pie fillings if made with a milk substitute; see listing of LACTOSE-FREE FOOD PRODUCTS for specific brands.

Most plain fruit desserts.

Fruits, fresh, frozen, dried, or canned; pure fruit juices.

Yogurt (contains some lactose, but may be tolerated).

Frogurt® and Colombo® Frozen Yogurt, frozen dessert yogurts (both contain some lactose, but may be tolerated by many individuals).

Tofutti® and Tofree®, frozen lactose-free tofu desserts.

Yodolo®, a new frozen fruit dessert.

AVOID OR USE SPARINGLY:

Commercial and homemade desserts prepared with milk and milk products.

Sherbet, ice cream, custard, pudding, instant pudding.

Ice cream bars.

Strained infant desserts.

Some baking mixes, most chocolate desserts.

Juice drinks if whey is added.

Reduced-calorie desserts made with a sugar substitute containing lactose.

FATS, OILS, AND NUTS

ACCEPTABLE CHOICES:

Butter, milk-free margarine, some diet imitation margarines. Some examples are Diet Imperial®, Shedd's Spread®, Mother's Brand®, Diet Mazola®, Willow Run Margarine®.

Salad dressings without milk, cream, or cheese; Kraft Miracle
   Whip®, and mayonnaise.
Yogurt dressings and yogurt dips, while not lactose-free, may
   be tolerated by many individuals.
Vegetable oils, shortenings.
Olives, bacon.
Nondairy cream and whipped toppings without lactose or milk
      solids added, such as Coffee Rich®, Borden's
      Cremora®, Carnation Coffeemate®.
Any nuts**
**In certain medical situations, nuts may be irritating to the
   gastrointestinal tract. Check with your physician and/or
   dietitian.

AVOID OR USE SPARINGLY:
Dairy and nondairy creamers containing lactose, whey, and
   milk solids.
Sour cream, cream cheese.
Margarine with lactose, whey, or milk solids.
Chip dips made with sour cream.
Sauces or salad dressing containing milk or lactose; creamy
   dressings.

MEATS AND MEAT SUBSTITUTES

ACCEPTABLE CHOICES:
Any meat, fish, poultry, and eggs, except those listed as
   containing lactose, whey, or milk solids.
Some canned or frozen entrees. See SECTION 9 for brand
   names.
Kosher prepared meat products.

Eckrich Ball Park® franks and other sausage products without milk solids. Armour Frankfurters®, Oscar Mayer Frankfurters®.

Soy meat substitutes.

Dried peas, beans, and lentils.

Peanut butter.

Natural aged cheese, ripened, such as Bleu, Brick, Cheddar, Colby, Edam, Gouda, Monterey, Parmesan, and Swiss (see Aging Time of Cheese located at the end of this section). Most of the lactose in cheese-making is removed in the whey when it is separated from the curd. In ripened cheese, the small amount of lactose entrapped in the curd is transformed into lactic acid, which does not require lactase for absorption as lactose does.

Cottage cheese, mozzerella, Neufchatel, and ricotta cheese, and other unripened cheese. These cheeses contain lactose, but may be tolerated in limited quantities.

Lifeline® low fat aged cheese; Formagg® cheese

AVOID OR USE SPARINGLY:

Breaded or creamed meat or egg dishes.

Many canned or frozen entrees. Most frozen "TV" dinners.

Most other lunch meats, sausage products, liver sausage, and frankfurters with cereal and/or milk solids added.

Cream cheese.

American processed cheese, cheese spreads, imitation cheese food. These products have milk solids added, and are not aged.

POTATOES AND STARCHES

ACCEPTABLE CHOICES:

Potatoes, white or red; sweet potatoes, yams.

Pastas, such as macaroni, noodles, spaghetti.

Rice, brown, white, or wild. Rice mixes, if lactose-free.

Macaroni and cheese, creamed and escalloped potatoes, and au gratin potatoes, if made with milk substitutes and natural aged cheese.

AVOID OR USE SPARINGLY:

Commercial creamed and escalloped potatoes, au gratin potatoes, most instant potatoes; homemade potato dishes, if made with milk or milk products.

Potatoes and starches made with milk, lactose, or whey.

Macaroni and cheese mixes.

SEASONINGS

ACCEPTABLE CHOICES:

Any plain spices and herbs.

Spice blends, without lactose.

Monosodium glutamate, if 100% pure.

AVOID OR USE SPARINGLY:

Condiments and some spice blends with lactose added. Check labels. Monosodium glutamate as an ingredient in these spice blends may not be 100% pure, but the amount of lactose likely to be included would be exceedingly small, especially considering the amount of spice blend likely to be used at one time.

SOUPS

ACCEPTABLE CHOICES:

Bouillon, broth, meat stock soups, vegetable soups.

Cream soups, bisques, and chowders if made with water or milk substitutes. See listings in SECTION 9 for specific soups which are lactose-free.

AVOID OR USE SPARINGLY:

Cream soups made with milk or cream, most canned or frozen cream soups.

Some canned and dehydrated soup mixes. Check labels.

SWEETS AND CANDIES

ACCEPTABLE CHOICES:

Sugar: brown, granulated, or powdered, made from cane and sugar beets. When "sugar" is listed on the label of prepared foods, it refers to cane or beet sugar, not lactose.

Corn syrup, dextrose (corn sugar).

Honey.

Jams, jellies, marmalades.

Hard candies; candy made without lactose, milk, margarine, or chocolate. White chocolate candies, if made without whey, lactose, or milk.

Sugar substitutes without lactose.

AVOID OR USE SPARINGLY:

Chocolate and cream candies, toffee, peppermint candy, butterscotch candy, molasses candies, caramels.

Sugar substitutes containing lactose, such as Equal® in tablet

form.   However, the amount in such products is very
small and may be tolerated in limited quantities.

VEGETABLES

ACCEPTABLE CHOICES:
Fresh, frozen, and canned vegetables without milk or milk
    products.
Some frozen vegetables in a packaged sauce. See SECTION 9
    for specific products which are lactose-free.

AVOID OR USE SPARINGLY:
Creamed or breaded vegetables, vegetables with lactose-
    containing margarines.
Vegetables in a cheese sauce.
Some frozen vegetables in a packaged sauce.

MISCELLANEOUS FOODS

ACCEPTABLE CHOICES:
Popcorn**; pretzels, many snack crackers. See SECTION 9
    for specific brands.
Mustard, catsup, pickles, olives.
Gravies and sauces made without milk or lactose.   See
    RECIPES.
Flavorings, extracts.
Soy sauce, Worcestershire sauce.
Wrigley's chewing gum, some other brands of gum.

AVOID OR USE SPARINGLY:
Some chewing gum.

Korn Kurls®, and some other snack chips.

Cream sauces, milk gravy.

Ascorbic acid tablets, citric acid mixtures containing lactose.

Any food containing MILK, LACTOSE, WHEY, OR MILK
    SOLIDS.

**In certain medical situations, popcorn may be irritating to the
    gastrointestinal tract. Check with your physician and/or
    dietitian.

AGING TIME OF CHEESE

Lactose is converted into lactic acid by the ripening or
aging process. A longer aging time will yield a reduced lactose
content. A cheese aged six months or more should be well
tolerated by most lactose-intolerant people, although cheese
aged for less time may be tried.

Soft unripened varieties:	Cottage Cheese	unripened
	Ricotta Cheese	unripened
	Cream Cheese	unripened
	Neufchatel	unripened
Firm unripened varieties:	Gjetost	unripened
	Mysost or Primost	unripened
	Mozzarella	unripened
Soft ripened varieties:	Brie	4-8 weeks
	Camembert	4-8 weeks
	Limburger	4-8 weeks
Semisoft ripened varieties:	Bel Paese	6-8 weeks
	Brick	2-4 mo.
	Muenster	1-8 weeks
	Port du Salut	6-8 weeks
Firm ripened varieties	Cheddar	1-12 mo.

	Colby	1-3 mo.
	Caciocavallo	3-12 mo.
	Edam	2-3 mo.
	Gouda	2-6 mo.
	Provolone	1-12 mo.
	Swiss	3-9 mo.
Very hard ripened varieties:	Parmesan	14 mo. to 2 years
	Romano	5-12 mo.
	Sap Sago	5 months+
Blue vein mold ripened :	Blue or Bleu	2-6 mo.
	Gorgonzola	3-12 mo.
	Roquefort	2-5 mo.
	Stilton	2-6 months

Source: United States Department of Agriculture
         Marketing Bulletin #17
         Cheese Buying Guide for Consumers, 1961

SELF-QUIZ

Directions: Underline the foods in the following menu which contain lactose, or which are likely to contain lactose. Assume no special preparation. The correct answers are given on the following page.

Day #1
Breakfast
Orange Juice
Soft Cooked Egg
Blueberry Muffin
Shedd's Spread®
Ovaltine

Lunch
Creamed Tuna on Toast
Olive Garnish
Carrots and Celery Sticks
Peach Slices
Chocolate Cookie
Skim Milk

Dinner
Baked Ham
Potatoes au Gratin
French Green Beans
Tossed Salad with
Creamy Dressing
Vienna Bread with Butter
Pumpkin Pie
Tea with Lemon

Day #2

Banana
Omelette
Biscuit
Butter
Coffee with CoffeeRich

Roast Beef and
American Cheese
 on French Bread
Sliced Tomato on Lettuce
Vanilla Shake

Breaded Veal Cutlet
Mashed Potatoes
Mixed Vegetables
Molded Fruit Salad
 Mayonnaise
Soft Rolls/Butter
Custard
Vitamite®

ANSWERS TO SELF-QUIZ

Day #1   Day #2
Breakfast
Orange Juice   Banana
Soft Cooked Egg   Omelette
Blueberry Muffin   Biscuit
Shedd's Spread®   Butter
Ovaltine   Coffee with Coffee Rich

Lunch
Creamed Tuna on Toast   Roast Beef and
Olive Garnish   American Cheese
Carrots and Celery Sticks   on French Bread
Peach Slices   Sliced Tomato on Lettuce
Chocolate Cookie   Vanilla Shake
Skim Milk

Dinner
Baked Ham   Breaded Veal Cutlet
Potatoes au Gratin   Mashed Potatoes
French Green Beans   Mixed Vegetables
Tossed Salad with   Molded Fruit Salad
Creamy Dressing   Mayonnaise
Vienna Bread with Butter   Soft Rolls /Butter
Pumpkin Pie   Custard
Tea with Lemon   Vitamite®

5

SETTING YOUR LACTOSE LEVEL

Treatment of lactose intolerance requires that lactose be restricted to an individual's tolerance level. This rarely means total elimination of lactose from the diet; although, in some instances total avoidance is necessary.

Lactose intolerance is an individual matter. One person may tolerate two cups of milk per day (24 grams of lactose), but another may tolerate only 1/4th cup milk (3 grams of lactose). Still another may tolerate none. There is no single "diet" which is imposed on every lactose-intolerant person. Each individual can and should determine for himself how much lactose he can tolerate, what forms of lactose are tolerated (whole milk or skim, etc.) and in what manner (milk in cooking or to drink). Review Nutritional Alternatives in SECTION 3 for suggestions.

PROCEDURE

The lactose level is established by the following method:

1. Follow a lactose-free diet carefully for 5 days. (See LACTOSE-RESTRICTED MENU PLANNER and

SAMPLE MENUS in SECTION 3.)   Symptoms should disappear. NOTE: If symptoms continue to persist, your problem may be more complex than simple lactose intolerance. If this should occur, try omitting caffeine and other gastrointestinal stimulants from your lactose-free test diet, such as coffee, decaffeinated coffee, tea, cola beverages, chocolate, and alcohol. If symptoms continue to persist, contact your physician for further investigation into your particular problem.

2. After you are symptom-free, add 1/4 cup of milk to breakfast while continuing with the otherwise lactose-free diet. Note any symptoms, such as diarrhea, cramping, or increased gas, during the next 24 hours.

3. If symptoms do not occur, increase milk to 1/2 cup on the following morning on the otherwise lactose-free diet.

4. Continue increasing milk by 1/4 cup increments until symptoms occur, then drop back to the previous day's milk intake.

5. Figure your lactose tolerance level by multiplying your milk intake in 1/4 cup servings by 3 grams each. (Milk contains 3 gram of lactose per 1/4 cup.) Example: You tolerated three 1/4-cup servings; multiply 3 servings x 3 grams lactose = 9 grams of lactose. This amount is equal to 3/4 cup of milk.

6. After you have established your lactose level for one meal (breakfast), begin the process again for lunch, taking 1/4 cup milk, while continuing to have the established amount of milk at breakfast. (If you wish to have less than the established amount at breakfast, do so, but be consistent.)

7. Again, increase by 1/4-cup increments until symptoms occur. Calculate your lactose level as before.

8. Repeat the process for dinner and/or other times milk is desired, but do so one meal at a time in 1/4 cup increments.

9. When you have completed your experiment, add up the amount of milk you are able to drink. Estimate how much milk you are likely to drink on a daily basis. If this amount is 2 cups or more (and if you are making the other recommended number of selections from the BASIC FOUR MEAL PLAN in SECTION 3), your diet is probably nutritionally adequate.
If, however, your tolerance and/or your predicted milk intake is less than 2 cups per day, your diet is likely to be inadequate in certain nutrients. Study the LACTOSE-RESTRICTED MENU PLANNER to see which foods can be used to provide the needed nutrients in spite of lactose intolerance.

10. See SECTION 10 for lactose figures for some foods which may be used in place of part of your milk intake in measured amounts. For example, 1/2 cup of

pudding may be used in place of 1/2 cup of milk, after you have determined you can tolerate 1/2 cup of milk.

ABOUT THE LACTOSE-RESTRICTED MENU PLANNER

The LACTOSE-RESTRICTED MENU PLANNER in SECTION 3 provides a guide for meal planning to allow for a wide selection of foods within lactose-restricted limitations. Specified numbers of selections are made from each of the four food lists. If milk products are limited, alternative suggestions are given, to provide adequate Vitamin A, riboflavin (Vitamin B_2), and calcium in the diet. The Sample Menus illustrate the use of the MENU PLANNER.

For the test period, use Ensure®, Isocal®, Soyamel®, Sustacal® or Vitamite®; thereafter, Lactaid® and other enzyme-treated milk may be used. (Lactaid® at the standard treatment level is 70-90% lactose-free, not 100%, and may confuse the results of the establishment of lactose-tolerance levels at this point.)

In preparing the foods for these menus, use butter or lactose-free margarine for all cooking, baking, and roasting. Use lactose-free bread or rolls. For additional beverage guidelines, see BEVERAGES in SECTION 4. All labels of packaged foods should be checked to be certain the meals for these five days are *lactose-free*.

AFTER THE TOLERANCE LEVEL IS SET

If you return to your usual diet, you will be consuming varying amounts of lactose, which will affect your ability to consistently tolerate the amount of milk you determined to be within your tolerance. Your diet may require adjustments in milk intake, depending on your usual consumption of other lactose-containing foods.

Unfortunately, most food companies do not have information available on the specific amounts of lactose in their products. Therefore, it is not possible to determine the total lactose content of a diet. Unless only lactose-free foods are eaten, the diet will vary from day to day in its lactose content, and the individual may vary in terms of symptoms.

6
GROCERY SHOPPING

In order to consistently avoid the uncomfortable symptoms of lactose intolerance, one must continually adhere to a lactose-restricted diet. To do so, the appropriate foods must be available. The following procedure is helpful for shopping for foods on a lactose-restricted diet.

SHOPPING POINTERS

1. Plan menus for one week, or other reasonable time span.
2. Prepare the shopping list.
>   Review recipes to determine what ingredients are needed.
>   Check the foods on hand, noting items needed.
3. Shop wisely, allowing sufficient time to read labels.

Shopping for groceries when one is on a lactose-restricted diet requires two important considerations: the shopper must be aware of which foods are likely to contain lactose, whey, or a form of milk solids, and the shopper must know how to read labels on the packaged food products and have the time to scrutinize the labels. A magnifying glass is useful for enlarging the small print on the labels.

Time can be saved by shopping for brands of foods which are listed in SECTION 9 as lactose-free, but even these labels should be checked periodically to determine if the manufacturer has added lactose, whey, or milk solids.

The local bakery should be able to supply information on lactose, whey, or milk additives in its items. The local Italian market or specialty foods shop may have lactose-free Italian ices. Jewish bakeries will have a variety of lactose-free breads and rolls.

Kosher meats, used by people practicing the Jewish faith, can be used by lactose-intolerant individuals with confidence. Kosher meat products contain no lactose, whey, or milk solids; an example is Kosher luncheon meat. The Kosher dietary rules prohibit the mixing of milk and meat at the same meal; therefore, any food which contains meat will never contain milk. (Of course, kosher milk dishes cannot be used by lactose-intolerant people.) An item labeled "Pareve" means the food can be eaten at either a dairy or meat meal; therefore it contains no milk. Kosher foods are denoted on the label by the word "kosher," or by the lower-case letter "k." Kosher foods may also show a U within a circle, Ⓤ, indicating the product has been approved by the Union of Orthodox Congregations.

Milk substitutes are available which are lactose-free. Some examples are Vitamite®, Soyamel®, Coffee Rich®, Ensure®, Ensure Plus® and Sustacal®. The Comparison Table shows some of the features of each. In addition, the enzyme-treated milks are available, and contain much less lactose than untreated milk.

PRODUCT	CALORIES/CUP	PROTEIN	TASTE	USE
Enzyme-treated Milk	80-170Cal	8-9gm	Slightly sweeter	Cooking or drinking
Soyamel®	130Cal	7gm	Similar to milk	Cooking or drinking
Ensure® Sustacal®	240 Cal	9 gm	Sweet	Drinking, dessert recipes, or shakes
Ensure Plus®	360 Cal	13 gm	Sweet	Drinking, dessert recipes or shakes
Vitamite®	100Cal	4gm	Same as milk	Cooking or drinking
Coffee Rich®	240 Cal	1 gm	Rich, creamy	On cereals or in coffee

ENZYME-TREATED MILK

Enzyme-treated milk can be used wherever milk would be used, as a drink, on cereal, in hot beverages, or in recipes that call for milk. Sugar in recipes may be reduced when using the slightly sweeter enzyme-treated milk.

The enzyme treatment involves lactase, the enzyme which splits milk sugar, thus allowing milk to be tolerated by lactose-intolerant people. It is available in powder or liquid form. Added to a quart of regular milk, the enzyme will split lactose into glucose and galactose, two sugars which are harmless to the lactose-intolerant person. This process takes 24 hours in the refrigerator. Enzyme-treated milk tastes slightly sweeter and richer than untreated milk.

Four to five drops of Lactaid® will convert approximately 70% of the lactose in a quart of milk. By doubling the amount of Lactaid® per quart, the lactose will be reduced by more than 90% in 24 hours. For greater than 99% lactose removal, use 12-15 drops per quart for 24 hours or 8-10 drops for 48 hours in the refrigerator before drinking.

Recently Lactaid® has begun to be marketed as ready-to-drink pre-treated milk. It is available in some areas of the country in the dairy sections of grocery stores in this convenient form. Lactaid® is also available in a high calcium ready-to-drink form. The company has also developed Lactaid® cheese slices which are available in some areas.

Lactaid® drops are available in some grocery stores, pharmacies, and specialty food stores, or they can be ordered by mail from the manufacturer, Lactaid, Inc., 600 Fire Road, P.O. Box 111, Pleasantville, NJ 08232.

Introductory samples of Lactaid® are available by sending a stamped self-addressed envelope to the manufacturer. For more information, Lactaid, Inc., has a toll-free telephone number for professional and consumer questions, 1-800-257-8650. In New Jersey, call 609-645-7500.

Lacteeze® is another lactase enzyme product used to digest the lactose (natural sugar) of milk and milk products into two simpler sugars (galactose and glucose). To use the Lacteeze® drops, just add 4 drops of Lacteeze® to one quart of milk, shake or stir to disperse the enzyme throughout the milk and store the container in the refrigerator for 24-48 hours. The milk will have a 70% lactose reduction after 24 hours and a 90% lactose reduction after 48 hours.

Lacteeze®-treated milk may be used in every way regular milk is, drinking, cooking, making ice cream, cheese, etc. It may be used to reduce lactose in fresh milk, reconstituted powdered milk, canned milk, whole, 2%, or skim milk.

Lacteeze® drops are not effective in buttermilk or yogurt, as these milk products are too acidic. Lacteeze® is available from Kingsmill Diet Foods, 1399 Kennedy Road, Scarborough, Ontario M1P 2L6. Telephone: (416) 755-1124.

SOY MILKS

Soy milks must be fortified with calcium in order to be nutritionally equivalent to milk. The flavor of soy milk is generally acceptable, but slightly "beany." It is often better accepted in a flavored beverage. Soy milk can also be used in cooking in place of whole milk. The recipe section contains recipes using these products.

Soy milk is made of soy solids, corn syrup, soy oil, sugar, with vitamins and minerals added to approach the nutritional content of milk. In selecting a soy milk, it is important to study the labels to determine how closely the nutrient content resembles milk. Soy milk is available at grocery stores, specialty food stores and pharmacies, or it can be ordered from the manufacturer.

A product which is nutritionally similar to milk is Soyamel®. It contains 240 mg calcium, .48 mg riboflavin, and 5.6 gm protein. Powdered Soyamel® is available in Regular, Fortified, and Lowfat forms, in 8-oz, 2-lb., and 20-lb. cartons. It is produced by Worthington Foods, 900 Proprietors Road, Worthington, Ohio 43085.

Another soy milk product is Soyagen®, a soy beverage powder which provides, in one cup: 120 mg calcium, .16 mg riboflavin, and 4.5 gm protein. This provides approximately half the calcium of milk. It is made by Loma Linda Foods, Riverside, CA 92515.

There are several products on the market which are merely flavored drinks made of soy; although many of these are lactose-free, they are not nutritionally equivalent to milk.

ENSURE® and SUSTACAL®

Ensure® and Sustacal® are two examples of lactose-free nutritional supplements which are good sources of calcium, protein, and calories, as well as many other nutrients. One 8-ounce cup of Sustacal® supplies approximately 240 calories,14 grams of protein, and 240 mg calcium. One 8-ounce cup of Ensure® supplies 250 calories, 9 grams of protein and 130 mg calcium. These products are designed primarily to increase calorie and nutrient intake, but can be used as a milk substitute if one can afford the extra calories. They taste much sweeter than milk, and come in a variety of flavors. Ensure Plus® is a similar product, but provides 360 calories per cup. It may be used where additional calories are needed.

The major ingredients of these products are water, sucrose (sugar), corn syrup, calcium caseinate, partially hydrogenated soy oil, soy protein isolate, sodium caseinate, potassium citrate and a host of vitamins and minerals.

Available at most pharmacies, Ensure® is produced by Ross Labs; Sustacal® is produced by Mead Johnson.

VITAMITE®

Vitamite® is a nondairy milk substitute which is found in the dairy case of many large food stores. One eight-ounce glass supplies 100 calories, 4 grams of protein, 20% of the daily calcium allowance, and 25% of the daily phosphorus allowance. It is made of water, corn syrup solids, vegetable fat and sodium caseinate. Vitamite® can be used wherever milk would be used, as a drink, on cereal, or in hot beverages, or in recipes that call for milk.

Vitamite® is also available as a powder in 7-1/2#, 25#,

or 50# bags. One pound of dry mix yields one gallon of Vitamite®. In view of the limited storage time for the liquid Vitamite® (approximately five days in the refrigerator), it would be advisable to obtain the powdered Vitamite® and keep a few days' supply mixed for use.

The cost of Vitamite® in either the liquid or powdered form is less than the price of regular milk. It is produced by Diehl Specialties International, 10800 Ambassador Boulevard, St. Louis, MO 63132-1792, and is distributed in the liquid form by local dairies. It can be ordered directly from the company in the dry mix form. Telephone (314) 994-1010.

Several new lactose-free beverages available from Diehl are Top "1" Chocolate Beverage and Top "1" Nogg, Top "1" Orange Creme, Top "1" Banana, Top "1" Vanilla, Top "1" Strawberry. These are not significant sources of calcium, but are very good-tasting. They also produce a frozen dessert mix which can be mixed with either Vitamite or water to produce a lactose-free frozen dessert. It can be easily made with a hand mixer and a home freezer compartment of a regular refrigerator.

COFFEE RICH®

Coffee Rich® is a nondairy creamer which contains no lactose, unlike many nondairy creamers which contain lactose or whey. One cup supplies 240 calories with 1 gram of protein, 32 grams of carbohydrate (sugar), and 16 grams of fat. Its use should be limited by persons on a low saturated fat or low cholesterol diet. It is relatively high in calories, low in protein, and high in saturated fat. It is not considered to be a nutritional replacement for milk; however, it is a very tasty product for use on cereal, or wherever cream is used.

Coffee Rich® can be used in recipes calling for milk or

cream, using the following conversion chart:

IN PLACE OF:	USE:
1 cup cream	1 cup Coffee Rich®
1 cup whole milk	1/2 cup Coffee Rich® + 1/2 cup water
1 cup skim milk	1/4 cup Coffee Rich® + 3/4 cup water

Coffee Rich® can be kept in the freezer until needed, then thawed in the refrigerator until it is completely fluid. It should be gently shaken before using. Refrigerated shelf life is approximately three weeks.

Coffee Rich® is located in the frozen food section at most grocery stores. Major ingredients include water, corn syrup, soy oil, and coconut oil. It is produced by Rich Products Corporation, Buffalo, NY 14213.

Other brands of lactose-free liquid creamers are available. Even though the label may state the product is non-dairy, check the fine print on the label to be sure it contains no lactose, whey, or milk solids.

READING LABELS

The lactose-intolerant individual needs to check the ingredient label on each item of packaged food which he purchases. *Many products contain lactose, even when they are not made from milk.*

The words on the label which indicate the presence of milk sugar or lactose are:

LACTOSE, WHEY, MILK, MILK SOLIDS,
DRY MILK SOLIDS
NONFAT DRY MILK POWDER

Ingredients are listed on labels in decreasing order according to weight. For example, in Swiss Miss® Hot Cocoa Mix, the label states:

> INGREDIENTS: Sugar, corn syrup solids, cocoa, processed with alkali, partially hydrogenated coconut oil, nonfat dry milk, whey, salt, etc.

This indicates the product contains two sources of lactose: nonfat dry milk and whey; and these ingredients are present in greater quantity than salt and less than sugar, corn syrup, cocoa, etc.

Another example: Mazola® Margarine

> INGREDIENTS. Liquid corn oil, partially hydrogenated corn oil, skim milk, salt, lecithin, etc.

This label lists skim milk as the third listed ingredient. It is present in the margarine in less quantity than the two oils, but in greater quantity than salt.

Lactose, whey, and milk solids are used in many packaged foods. It is helpful to be aware of the types of products in which these lactose-containing culprits may be found.

LACTOSE

When the term lactose appears on a label, it indicates a specific sugar has been added to the product in question. Lactose occurs naturally only in milk and milk products, but may be added to many foods having no association with milk. When the term sugar appears on a label, it refers to sucrose, which is cane or beet sugar, not lactose.

Lactose has two characteristics which make it desirable for use in commercial food production:

1. It dissolves easily.
2. It is less sweet than other sugars.

For example, lactose is used in some instant iced tea mixes to permit quick dissolving, and in Chinese restaurants mixed with monosodium glutamate for the same reason.

Lactose as an added ingredient may be present in French fried potatoes, baby foods, party dips, ice cream, pie fillings and bakery products. It is also found in dried foods, such as soups, instant potatoes, some instant breakfast drinks and powdered soft drinks and is used as a filler in many tablets and capsules. Sugar substitutes may also contain small amounts of lactose.

Incidently, lactic acid, lactate, lactylate, lactalbumin, lactoglobulin, and calcium compounds sometimes are mentioned on food labels; they do not contain lactose, and will not cause symptoms for the lactose-intolerant person.

WHEY

Whey is the greenish-yellow fluid drained from the vat after the protein portion of milk is made into cheese. Fluid whey is mainly lactose, although there is a small amount of protein remaining.

Since anti-pollution laws prevent dumping whey into rivers and sewerage systems, cheese manufacturers look for ways to use whey. It is sold to food companies for use in their products, thus adding hidden lactose.

Whey is used in a variety of products, such as wines, snack drinks, some milk substitutes, imitation milks and various liquid meals. One example of a carbonated beverage of the soft drink type containing whey is a Swiss product called Rivella®. It is a sparkling, crystal clear, herbal drink made of whey, and contains a significant amount of lactose. It is not yet available in this country, but plans are being made to market it and similar products here.

Whey can also be found in high protein beverages, frozen desserts, syrups and candies, especially caramels.

The dairy industry has the technology available for producing lactose-modified milk and milk products, including lactase-treated whey, which could then be used by the lactose-intolerant individual. As of now, one must assume whey is mainly lactose.

MILK SOLIDS

Milk solids, including nonfat dry milk and dry milk powder, are terms indicating milk with the water removed. The lactose remains in the solid particles.

Milk solids are used in many products to improve nutritive value, taste, color, and texture. They are found in many types of foods, including breads, rolls, sandwich buns, biscuits, muffins, sweet rolls, pancakes, doughnuts, waffles, margarine, casserole mixes, macaroni and cheese mixes, instant potatoes, cakes and cookies, baking mixes, instant pudding mixes, sauces, cold cuts and hot dogs, cream soups, processed cheese, dried creamers, weight reduction formulas, instant chocolate drinks, etc.

SUMMARY

In summary, lactose is found primarily in milk and milk-containing foods. These foods will not state lactose on the label, since it occurs naturally in milk and in foods made with milk. Lactose is added to many products, as described above, in the form of

> LACTOSE
> WHEY
> MILK
> MILK SOLIDS, DRY MILK SOLIDS
> NONFAT DRY MILK POWDER

The lactose-intolerant person is advised to be aware of these ingredients in packaged foods, and to avoid them as necessary. The degree of lactose intolerance varies from one individual to another. One individual may not tolerate lactose in any food, while another individual may be able to consume several lactose-containing foods per day. Being aware of such foods will enable the lactose-intolerant person to limit his intake of lactose to the point of preventing symptoms.

7

DINING AWAY FROM HOME

Dining away from home while attempting to adhere to a lactose-restricted diet presents a challenge. There are many situations in which problems can occur: traveling by car or by plane, dining in a variety of restaurants and fast-food establishments, being confined to a hospital or nursing home, and eating meals in a school setting.

Adhering to the diet limitations is worth the effort. Being away from home is much more enjoyable when one is free of symptoms of lactose intolerance. Lactase pills may be useful in preventing or minimizing symptoms when dining away from home in the event that lactose is inadvertently consumed. The most certain defense, however, is avoidance of lactose. Lactase pills are discussed in SECTION 3.

AUTOMOBILE TRAVEL

Traveling by car allows for food to be taken along to replace or to supplement restaurant meals. Aged cheese, various crackers and bread, milk-free cookies, canned lactose-free nutritional supplements, such as Ensure® or Sustacal®, can be carried or purchased in grocery stores or pharmacies along the way. Other lactose-free foods for travel include fresh fruits and juice, raw vegetables, soft drinks, and other lactose-free foods. Sandwiches may be taken along, with ham, beef, chicken, turkey or other plain meat as a filling. Also, canned tuna fish, kosher or lactose-free luncheon meats, or peanut butter may be used. Mayonnaise is lactose-free; boiled dressings should be checked for lactose content, although Kraft Miracle Whip® is lactose-free. Meats, fish, mayonnaise and salad dressings require refrigeration.

PLANE TRAVEL

Airlines usually require advance notice and possibly a physician's order for a modified diet to be served on the plane. This should be discussed with the airline's special services department as soon as flight arrangements are made.

RESTAURANTS

Dining in a restaurant presents a challenge. Ingredient labels are not accessible; therefore, if total avoidance of lactose is necessary, one must assume any questionable product, such as bread or margarine, does contain lactose. If a small amount of lactose is tolerated, then only the more significant sources of lactose need to be avoided, such as cream soups or escalloped potatoes.

Kosher Jewish restaurants will be reliable for lactose-free foods because of the dietary rules forbidding milk-containing foods to be served at a meal which contains meat.

Chinese restaurants require caution because of the practice of adding monosodium glutamate (MSG) to nearly all foods. The monosodium glutamate is mixed with lactose powder to promote rapid dissolving and thickening. Therefore, many Chinese dishes can have surprisingly high levels of lactose. Most Chinese restaurants offer the option of requesting that no MSG be added; however, some foods are prepared with MSG during cooking, so it may not be possible to avoid it in these cases. Such foods include sweet and sour entrees and Egg Foo Yung. The staff can provide information on MSG, and hence lactose, in their establishment.

FAST-FOOD RESTAURANTS

Fast-food restaurant menus are rather limited, but lactose-free foods can be found here, too. Avoid the items which are most likely to contain lactose, such as French fries (they may be soaked in a lactose solution in the freezing process), cheese (it will most likely be processed, not natural aged), breaded items, such as fried chicken and fried fish squares, milkshakes (even if they are not made with real ice cream), and, of course, ice cream.

Suggested fast-food selections include the salad bar (without the shredded cheese and creamy dressing), baked potato (with real butter, not sour cream), and hamburger (no cheese; the small amount of milk solids in the bun may be tolerated). Soft drinks, fruit juice, tea, or coffee may be selected as the beverage. See SECTION 9 for listings of lactose-free foods available at Burger King® and McDonald's®.

HOSPITALS AND NURSING HOMES

By contacting the dietitian or food service director in advance, a lactose-restricted diet can be served to the individual without interruption, thus avoiding symptoms. The facility may be able to obtain the milk substitutes, or may ask for them to be supplied by the patient or his family.

SCHOOL FOOD SERVICE OR SACK LUNCH

School food service presents a similar problem. It may be possible to make arrangements for a lactose-restricted diet by contacting the school food service director, or it may be advisable to plan on carrying a sack lunch. Sandwiches can be made of lactose-free bread and a variety of fillings, such as peanut butter, natural aged cheese, sliced meats and poultry, or meat salads. The use of meat mixtures and tuna salad will depend on availability of refrigeration.

Fresh fruits and raw vegetables, pickles and olives can be included. Milk-free cookies or cakes prepared from basic lactose-free ingredients can be used. If ready-to-eat products or packaged mixes are included, check labels to avoid lactose, whey, and milk solids.

Milk substitutes, such as Soyamel®, Vitamite®, or enzyme-treated milk, such as LactAid®, can be carried in a thermos. Others can be purchased in single serving cans, such as Ensure® and Sustacal®.

OFFICE PARTIES

Office parties and other social events present special problems. Usually the menu is limited to a few items. Often, they are prepared by friends or family, who may be unaware of the lactose problem.

For example, at a monthly office birthday party, the menu included chocolate cake, ice cream, and fruit punch made with sherbet. Ellen, who had rather severe lactose intolerance, knew she could tolerate none of these lactose-containing foods. She debated whether she should not attend the party or put herself in the embarrassing (to her) situation of avoiding the food. She decided to join in the party, take along a few lactose-free cookies from her desk drawer, and have a cup of tea. When her co-workers asked her (as co-workers will) why she wasn't eating the dessert, she said she was on a lactose-free diet, and gave a brief explanation. At the next party she was surprised and delighted to find angelfood cake topped with berries served with fruit juice for the refreshments.

Many people feel embarrassed about following a modified diet in a social situation. The preparing and sharing of food is an age-old way of showing concern and affection. When the dieter rejects the food, he worries that he may offend the food giver, so he may risk the discomfort of lactose intolerance symptoms instead. However, usually a brief explanation to the host or hostess will be sufficient to promote an understanding of the situation.

MENU SUGGESTIONS

Following are suggested foods to select and to avoid when eating meals away from home. These suggestions can be adapted to various dining settings, such as restaurants, hospitals and nursing homes, school food service, office parties, social occasions, etc.

APPETIZERS

Select fruits and juices, shrimp, or crabmeat cocktail; broths or bouillons.

Avoid most soups;   herring or other fish marinated in sour cream.

ENTREES

Select plain meats, fish or poultry, prepared without added ingredients. Request real butter for broiled entrees, or request no butter or margarine be added. Select entrees in a tomato sauce, such as meat sauce and spaghetti.

Avoid breaded entrees or those dipped in a batter, casseroles and mixed dishes, although meats in a tomato sauce will usually be lactose-free. Avoid deep fried and battered meats, fish, chicken, or shrimp, frankfurters and sausage products. Avoid cheese dishes; they may contain milk and processed cheese. Also, avoid entrees in cream sauces and milk gravies.

ACCOMPANIMENTS

Select fresh lettuce salads (with careful choice of ingredients at a salad bar), plain unbuttered vegetables, oil and vinegar coleslaw, baked potato with real butter. Select rice, noodles, and spaghetti. Yogurt dressing may be used if tolerated.

Avoid creamy coleslaw, French fried potatoes, French fried onion rings, au gratin potatoes and vegetables, cottage cheese and ricotta cheese (unless you have determined a tolerance for it). Avoid foods made with American processed cheese.

BREAD AND ROLLS

Select crusty rolls, French, Vienna, or Italian bread, Jewish breads, Kaiser rolls, rye bread, rusk, or Premium® or Zesta® saltines. Crackers may be in individual packets, with ingredients listed.

Avoid soft breads and rolls, hamburger buns, cheese breads, biscuits, coffeecakes, doughnuts, waffles and pancakes, muffins and quick breads.

DESSERTS

Select fresh fruit, gelatin, or most fruit pies. Select angelfood cake, fruit ice made with juice or water; yogurt, if tolerated. Some restaurants are also offering Frogurt®or other frozen yogurt desserts.

Avoid cakes, cookies, ice cream, sherbet, soufflés, cheesecake, pudding, custard, whipped desserts, and whipped topping. Avoid chocolate desserts.

BEVERAGES

Select coffee, tea (not instant), Postum®, water, fruit juices, carbonated beverages (except special European health drinks, namely Rivella®), lemonade if fresh or frozen, alcoholic beverages (except wines with sugar added, and alcoholic beverages mixed with cream or ice cream). Select buttermilk, if tolerated.

Avoid milk, milkshakes, hot chocolate, and other milk or cream drinks. In instances of lactose intolerance associated with other gastrointestinal disease conditions, it may be advisable to avoid caffeine-containing beverages and other gastrointestinal stimulants, such as coffee, decaffeinated coffee, tea, colas, chocolate, and alcohol. Decaffeinated teas are usually well tolerated. Avoid cordials and liqueurs.

BREAKFAST ITEMS

Select plain eggs prepared in real butter; bacon, ham, and rye toast.

Avoid scrambled eggs and omelettes, pancakes, waffles, biscuits, sweet rolls, muffins. Avoid cooked cereals which may be prepared with milk. Avoid dry cereals unless a milk substitute is available.

RESTAURANT MENUS

Fresh Fruit Cup
Broiled Filet of Sole with Butter and Lemon
Boiled Red Jacket Potatoes
Steamed Broccoli
Dinner Salad with French Dressing
Crusty Rolls with Butter
Cherry Pie
Coffee or Tea
***

Shrimp Cocktail with Seafood Sauce
Broiled Breast of Chicken
White and Wild Rice
Steamed Asparagus Spears
Dinner Salad with Oil and Vinegar Dressing
French Bread with Butter
Fresh Melon in Season
Coffee or Tea
***

Sack Lunch Menu

Shaved Ham on Rye Bun
with Lettuce and Mayonnaise
Pickles, Carrot Sticks, and Celery Sticks.
Fresh Fruit
Lactose-free Cookies
Orange Juice or Milk Substitute
***

Menu for the Office Party

Natural Aged Cheddar and Swiss Cheese
Assorted Crackers
Apple Slices, Orange Sections, and Pineapple Spears
Coffee or Tea
***

Angelfood Cake Wedges
with Sliced Strawberries
Lemonade
Coffee or Tea
***

Fast-Food Salad Bar
    Lettuce, spinach, endive, romaine, and other greens, tossed with carrots, chopped onions, chopped green peppers, garbanzo beans, chopped egg, bacon bits, mushrooms, sliced tomatoes, sliced radishes, sliced cucumbers, served with French or Italian dressing and assorted crackers (check the label).

8

RECIPES

The RECIPE SECTION includes recipes from the authors' recipe collection, adapted here for lactose restriction. Also included are recipes from several milk substitute manufacturers, illustrating how various lactose free products can be used. The recipes are chosen especially to show how to prepare several types of recipes without using milk or other lactose-containing ingredients. The index for the RECIPE SECTION is located in SECTION 10.

Standard cookbooks contain many recipes which are lactose-free. Most entrees, side dishes, salads, vegetables, appetizers and desserts are made without any milk. For example, the following menu was taken from *Betty Crocker's New Picture Cookbook* to illustrate this point:

Roast Beef, page 300
Baked Potato with Butter and Chives, page 426
French Cut Green Beans, page 411
Perfection Salad with Mayonnaise, page 378
Double Quick Dinner Rolls, page 107
Lemon Meringue Pie, page 353

These recipes, prepared as written, are essentially lactose-free. The lactose-intolerant individual can find many more such recipes in any standard cookbook which can be used in his diet.

The recipes included here serve as examples of ways to alter other similar recipes. Recipes can be altered by referring to the list of substitutions for lactose-containing ingredients. There are some limitations when substituting one ingredient for another, and some trial and error may be necessary in order to find the preferred substitute ingredient.

Some recipes call for yogurt or buttermilk, either of which is usually tolerated by lactose-intolerant people.

SUBSTITUTIONS

In place of:

Cream, half & half, 10-12% butterfat, 1 cup

Use: 1-1/2 tablespoons butter or milk-free margarine plus about 7/8 cup milk substitute, or 1/2 cup Coffee Rich® plus 1/2 cup milk substitute.

Cream, coffee, at least 20% butterfat, 1 cup

Use: 3 tablespoons butter or milk-free margarine, plus about 7/8 cup milk substitute.

Cream, whipping, heavy, 36-40% butterfat, 1 cup

Use: 1/3 cup butter or milk-free margarine plus about 3/4 cup milk substitute. This substitution cannot be used for whipping.

Cream, sour, 1 cup

Use: 3 tablespoons butter or milk-free margarine plus 7/8 cup buttermilk or yogurt.

Or use: Soyamel® Special Sour Kreem recipe.

Milk, whole, 1 cup

Use: 1 cup soy milk, or Vitamite®, or Lactaid®, or 1 cup coconut milk, or 1 cup almond milk, or 1 cup fruit juice, or 1 cup potato water, depending on the recipe and resulting flavor.

Or use: 1 cup Ensure® or Sustacal® and decrease sugar in recipe.

Milk, whole, 1 cup

Use: 1 cup water plus 1-1/2 teaspoons butter or milk-free margarine.

Note: Butter contains a trace of lactose; it is tolerated by most lactose-intolerant persons.

Buttermilk and yogurt can be used interchangeably in most recipes, and are tolerated by many lactose-intolerant persons.

APPETIZERS

Many lactose-free appetizers can be found in regular cookbooks by selecting those which do not contain sour cream, cream cheese, processed cheese, milk, cream, or whipped cream. Some examples of lactose-free appetizers are: rumaki, caviar on milk-free crackers, raw vegetables, shaved ham or turkey party sandwiches on milk-free bread.

Cheese-containing appetizers may be used, if natural aged cheese is used in place of American processed cheese.

Cheese Nuggets
1 cup shredded Edam cheese
2 tablespoons finely chopped celery
1/8 teaspoon dry mustard
2 tablespoons milk substitute or ale

Combine all ingredients. Shape into small balls and roll in finely chopped parsley.

Cucumber Dip   Lacteeze Recipes
1/2 cucumber, diced finely and drained
1/2 cup enzyme-treated milk
3/4 cup mayonnaise
2 tablespoons lemon juice
2 tablespoons chopped parsley
1/2 teaspoon salt
1/4 teaspoon pepper
1 teaspoon sugar
     Combine all ingredients and mix well. Cover and chill until serving time. Serve as dip for vegetables or as a dressing for salad. Makes 2 cups.

Deviled Dip   Weight Watcher's Party Cookbook
1 cup plain unflavored yogurt
1 tablespoon dehydrated onion flakes
1 tablespoon prepared mustard
1 tablespoon steak sauce
Salt and hot sauce to taste
     In bowl combine all ingredients; mix well. Cover and chill. When ready to serve, transfer mixture to serving bowl. Makes 8 servings. Serve with vegetables and fruits.

Dill Dressing   Weight Watcher's Party Cookbook
1 cup plain unflavored yogurt
2 tablespoons minced fresh parsley
1 teaspoon dill weed or 1 tablespoon chopped dill.
1/4 teaspoon garlic powder
1/4 teaspoon onion powder
1/4 teaspoon white pepper
     Combine all ingredients in small bowl; chill. Makes 8 servings. Serve with fresh vegetables.

BEVERAGES

Almond Mocha
Mead Johnson
1 cup milk substitute
1 teaspoon Postum® (or instant coffee)
1 tablespoon boiling water
1/8 tsp almond extract
2 teaspoons sugar, or to taste

Dissolve Postum® in boiling water. Add milk substitute, almond extract and sugar. Stir well and serve. Makes 1 serving.

Banana Blush
1 cup milk substitute
1 small banana
1 teaspoon vanilla extract
1 teaspoon sugar, or to taste

Place banana and milk substitute in blender and blend until smooth and frothy. Add vanilla extract and sugar to taste. Add a few drops of cherry, strawberry, or cranberry juice to provide blush, blend briefly. Serve immediately (beverage darkens if allowed to stand).

Banana Soyamel® Shake
       Soyamel® Facts and Recipes
Mix in electric blender:
8 level tablespoons Soyamel® powder
2 cups water
1 large banana
1 tablespoon honey or sugar
1/2 teaspoon vanilla
       One tablespoon malt may be added if desired for malt flavor. To make an extra thick drink, half of the reconstituted Soyamel® can be frozen, then added to the rest of the Soyamel® and other ingredients at time of mixing. Any frozen fruit may be added to Soyamel® for a delicious drink. Try freezing canned peaches, pears, etc. in a refrigerator tray and then add to Soyamel® in a blender or liquifier to make a delicious frozen drink.

Banana Strawberry Shake
       Soyamel® Facts and Recipes
1-1/2 cups water
1/2 cup lowfat Soyamel® powder
1 package frozen strawberries (10 oz.), partially thawed
1 large banana, cut into 1-inch pieces
       Blend water and lowfat Soyamel® in a blender. Add undrained strawberries and banana. Blend until smooth. Serve immediately or refrigerate. Yields 3-1/2 cups.
Variation: Substitute 1/4 cup orange juice concentrate for strawberries for a Banana Orange Shake.

Creamy Fruit Drink   Mead Johnson

1-1/2 cups sweetened milk substitute, such as Sustacal® or
     Ensure®
1/4 teaspoon vanilla extract
1/4 teaspoon cinnamon
1/2 cup or 1 small can of sliced peaches in heavy syrup
3 drops yellow food coloring.

Pour sweetened milk substitute in blender. Add peaches, vanilla extract, cinnamon, and food coloring. Blend thoroughly. Pour into 2 glasses; chill.

Creamy Raspberry Cooler

1 cup milk substitute
1/2 cup raspberry yogurt

Place milk substitute and yogurt into blender. Blend at high speed. Pour and serve. Makes 1 serving - 12 ounces.

Variation: Try your own favorite flavored yogurt.

Eggnog

1 cup sweetened milk substitute, such as Ensure® or
     Sustacal®
1 large egg
1/2 teaspoon vanilla extract
1/2 teaspoon rum extract
Dash nutmeg

Blend milk substitute and egg. Flavor to taste with vanilla extract, rum extract, and nutmeg. Pour and serve. Makes 1 serving.

Hot Cocoa
        Lighter Chocolate Desserts - Hershey's
2 tablespoons Hershey's Cocoa
3 tablespoons sugar
1/4 cup hot water
1 1/2 cups enzyme-treated milk or milk substitute
1/8 teaspoon vanilla
        Blend cocoa and sugar in small saucepan; gradually add hot water. Cook over medium heat, stirring constantly, until mixture boils; boil and stir for 2 minutes. Add milk; heat thoroughly. Stir occasionally; do not boil. Remove from heat; add vanilla. Serve hot. Two 7-ounce servings.

Soyamel® Coconut Milk
        Soyamel® Facts and Recipes
        Mix Soyamel® according to directions using 6 level tablespoons to 2 cups water.
To the 2 cups of Soyamel® add 2 level tablespoons of grated or ground coconut. Mix thoroughly in electric blender or mixer. Chill and serve. If desired, this mixture may be strained before serving and the larger particles of coconut will be removed, but the flavor is still there. Some people like the drink sweeter; bland honey may be used.

BREADS

Many yeast bread recipes are milk-free when a crispy crust is desired, such as in Italian, French, and Vienna breads. They require no modification in the standard cookbooks, simply a review of the ingredients to be sure all are lactose free.

Yeast bread recipes contain milk or milk solids when a soft crust is desired, such as in sweet rolls, in some dinner rolls and breads. To modify the recipe, the milk solids can be omitted; water, potato water, or milk substitutes can be use in place of liquid milk in yeast bread recipes.

Quick bread recipes frequently contain milk as the liquid portion of the recipe. Alternative liquids are soy milk, Vitamite®, Lactaid®, fruit juices, or water. In addition, butter or milk free margarines should be used.

Biscuits
2 cups flour, sifted
3 teaspoons baking powder
1 teaspoon salt
1/3 cup vegetable oil
2/3 cup milk substitute, not a sweetened milk substitute

Heat oven to 475°F (very hot). Mix dry ingredients well in bowl. Pour oil and milk substitute into measuring cup (do not stir together). Pour all at once into flour mixture. Stir with fork until mixture cleans sides of bowl and forms a ball. To knead: turn onto waxed paper; lift paper by one corner and fold dough in half; press down firmly; pull paper back. Repeat until dough looks smooth. Pat or roll 1/2" thick between 2 sheets of waxed paper. Cut with unfloured biscuit cutter. Place on ungreased baking sheet. Bake 10-12 minutes, or until golden brown. Serve hot with milk-free margarine or butter and jelly, honey, jam, or pure syrup. Makes 16 biscuits.

Buttermilk Pancakes
1 egg
1-1/4 cups buttermilk
2 tablespoons vegetable oil or melted milk-free margarine
1-1/4 cups flour, sifted
1 tablespoon sugar
1 teaspoon baking powder
1/2 teaspoon baking soda
1/2 teaspoon salt

Blend egg, milk and oil. Blend dry ingredients together. Add to liquids; beat with fork until all flour is moistened. Batter will be slightly lumpy. Grease heated griddle, if necessary. To test, sprinkle with drops of water. When water sizzles, griddle heat is just right. Pour batter from pitcher or tip of large spoon in pools slightly apart, for perfectly round cakes. Turn pancakes as soon as they are puffed and full of bubbles, but before bubbles break. Turn and brown on other side. Serve immediately with butter and syrup. If necessary, keep pancakes hot by placing between folds of warm towel in warm oven. (Don't stack them.) Makes 16 4" pancakes.

Muffins

1 egg
1/2 cup milk substitute or 1/2 cup fruit juice
1/4 cup vegetable oil or melted milk-free margarine
1-1/2 cups flour, sifted
1/2 cup sugar
2 teaspoons baking powder
1/2 teaspoon salt

Heat oven to 400°F (moderately hot). Grease bottoms of muffin cups or use paper baking cups. Beat egg with fork. Stir in milk substitute or fruit juice and oil. Blend dry ingredients; stir in just until flour is moistened. Batter should be lumpy. Do not overmix. Fill muffin cups 2/3 full. Bake 20-25 minutes, or until golden brown. Muffins will have gently rounded tops. Loosen immediately with a spatula. Serve warm. Makes 12 medium muffins.

Sweet Milk Pancakes

Make Buttermilk Pancakes (above)--except substitute Lactaid®, Vitamite®, or a soy milk for buttermilk, add 2 teaspoons more baking powder, and omit baking soda. OPTIONAL: For extra lightness, beat egg yolk, add milk substitute, etc. Fold in stiffly beaten egg white.

Waffles

Toastmaster Waffle Baker

1-3/4 cups sifted flour
2 teaspoons baking powder
1/2 teaspoon salt
1 tablespoon sugar
3 beaten egg yolks
1-1/2 cups milk substitute
7 tablespoons melted shortening or cooking oil
3 stiff-beaten egg whites

Sift together dry ingredients in a large mixing bowl. Combine egg yolks and milk; stir into dry ingredients. Stir in cooking oil. Carefully fold in egg whites, leaving a few little fluffs. Do not overmix. Bake in preheated waffle baker.

CAKES

Angelfood cake and true sponge cake recipes do not contain milk. Most other cake recipes include milk and/or other milk products. Alternative liquids include soy milk, Vitamite®, Lactaid®, fruit juice, and water. If the recipe calls for sour cream, Soyamel® Special Sour Kreem can be used. See the Substitution List at the beginning of the RECIPE SECTION for other alternatives for lactose-containing ingredients in cake recipes. A few cake recipes are included here as examples of lactose-free products.

Chocolate Cupcakes
Lighter Chocolate Desserts - Hershey's
1 1/2 cups unsifted all-purpose flour
1 cup sugar
1/4 cup Hershey's Cocoa
1 teaspoon baking soda
1/2 teaspoon salt
1 cup water
1/4 cup plus 2 tablespoons vegetable oil
1 tablespoon vinegar
1 teaspoon vanilla

Combine flour, sugar, cocoa, baking soda and salt in medium mixing bowl. Add water, oil, vinegar and vanilla. Beat with mixer, wire whisk or wooden spoon until batter is smooth and ingredients are well blended. Pour batter into paper-lined muffin pans (2 1/2 inches in diameter), filling each 2/3 full. Bake at 375⁰ for 16 to 18 minutes or until tester inserted in center comes out clean. Remove to wire rack; cool completely. Frost as desired. About 1 1/2 dozen cupcakes.

Easy Coconut Cake
        Soyamel® Facts and Recipes
2 cups all-purpose flour
1-1/2 cups sugar
3 teaspoons baking powder
1 teaspoon salt
1/2 cup vegetable shortening
1 cup reconstituted Soyamel®
2 eggs
1-1/2 teaspoons vanilla flavoring

        Sift dry ingredients together in a mixer bowl. Add shortening and 2/3 cup reconstituted Soyamel®. Mix slowly until flour is dampened. Beat at medium-high speed for 2 minutes. Scrape bowl. Add remaining Soyamel®, eggs, and vanilla. Beat 2 minutes longer at medium-high speed. Bake in two greased and floured 9 x 1-1/2 inch round pans at 350°F. for 35 minutes. Cool layers for 15 minutes. Remove from pans onto cooling racks. Allow to cool completely. Frost cake with your favorite white icing and sprinkle generously with coconut. Decorate with mandarin orange sections if desired.

Orange Cake
3 cups cake flour, sifted
3/4 teaspoon salt
3-1/2 teaspoons baking powder
Rind of 1 orange, grated
1-1/2 cups sugar
3/4 cup butter or milk-free margarine
3 eggs
1/2 cup orange juice
1/2 cup water
2 tablespoons lemon juice

Preheat oven to 375. Sift together cake flour, salt and baking powder. Set aside. Combine grated orange rind with sugar. Add to butter or milk-free margarine; cream together until light and fluffy. Beat in eggs one at a time. Mix juices and water together Set aside.

Add the flour mixture in 3 parts to the butter or milk-free margarine mixture, alternately with the juice mixture. Stir the batter after each addition until smooth. Bake the cake about 30 minutes in 3 layer pans with greased bottoms. When the cake is cool, spread Orange Filling between the layers. Frost with Orange Icing.

Orange Filling
1/2 cup orange juice
1/3 cup water
1/2 cup sugar
2 tablespoons all-purpose flour
1/8 teaspoon salt
3 beaten egg yolks, or 1 egg and 1 yolk
1/2 teaspoon grated orange rind

Stir and cook in the top of a double boiler over--not in-- boiling water, until thick. Cool the filling before spreading between the cake layers.

Orange Icing
1 cup granulated sugar
1 tablespoon white corn syrup
1/8 teaspoon cream of tartar
1/2 cup water
2 beaten egg whites
1/4 cup powdered sugar
1 teaspoon grated orange rind
1 tablespoon orange juice or 3/4 teaspoon vanilla

Place sugar, corn syrup, cream of tartar, and water in saucepan and stir over heat until dissolved. Cover and cook about 3 minutes or until the steam has washed down any crystals that may have formed on the sides of the pan. Uncover and cook to 238° to 240° without stirring. Pour the syrup in a slow stream over the beaten egg whites. Beat for 10 minutes. Add sugar, orange rind, and juice or vanilla. Beat the icing to a spreading consistency.

Red Raspberry Flan

Soyamel® Facts and Recipes

1-1/4 cups reconstituted Soyamel®

1/3 cup sugar

3 eggs

1 teaspoon vanilla

1/8 teaspoon salt

2/3 cup flour

3 cups fresh or frozen drained red raspberries

1/3 cup sugar

Place first 6 ingredients in a blender in the order listed while blending at medium speed. Blend at high speed 1 minute. Pour a thin layer of batter into a greased 1-1/2 to 2 quart flame-proof casserole. Cook at low heat until batter sets. (If you have no flame-proof casserole, place dish in the oven at 350°F. until set.) Remove casserole from heat. Spread red raspberries over set batter. Sprinkle with 1/3 cup sugar. Pour remaining batter over raspberries. Bake at 350°F. for 60 to 70 minutes until top is lightly browned. Serve while slightly warm.

Southern Pecan Peach Shortcake
        Soyamel® Facts and Recipes
1-1/2 cups flour
3 teaspoons baking powder
1/4 teaspoon soda
1/2 teaspoon salt
1/2 cup brown sugar, packed
1/3 cup vegetable shortening
2/3 cup chopped pecans
3/4 cup reconstituted Soyamel®
1 egg
4 cups sliced fresh peaches, sweetened (or canned or frozen peaches)
Special Sour Kreem (see recipe in Sauce Section)
1/2 cup brown sugar, packed

        Into a large bowl, sift the flour, baking powder, soda and salt. Cut in 1/2 cup brown sugar and shortening. Add pecans. Combine Soyamel® and egg. Add to dry ingredients. Stir with a fork till just blended --do not overmix.

        Place in a greased round 9 x 1-1/2 inch layer pan. Bake at 375°F. for 25 minutes. Split the cake into two layers while still warm. Place bottom layer on a serving platter. Top with half the peaches. Place top layer over peaches. Top with remaining peaches. Spoon Special Sour Kreem over the peaches. Sprinkle 1/2 cup brown sugar over the Kreem. If desired, garnish with fresh mint. Use any desired fruit in place of the peaches or a combination of peaches and raspberries, blueberries or strawberries. Serves 8.

COOKIES

There are many cookie recipes which do not contain milk or lactose. A few substitutions will allow nearly any cookie recipe to be adapted to the lactose-restricted diet.

If margarine is needed, use a milk-free margarine, real butter, or vegetable oil. Some recipes call for buttermilk, which may be tolerated by many individuals. Fruit juice or a milk substitute may be used in those recipes calling for milk. For cookies calling for one cup of sour cream, use 3 tablespoons of butter or milk-free margarine plus 7/8 cup of yogurt, or use the recipe for Special Sour Kreem in the Sauce Section.

Chocolate Drop Cookies
 No-bake quickies.
2 cups sugar
1/2 cup butter or milk-free margarine
1/2 cup cocoa powder
1/2 cup milk substitute
3 cups quick-cooking rolled oats
1/2 cup chopped nuts
1 teaspoon vanilla
 Mix sugar, butter or milk-free margarine, cocoa powder, and milk substitute in saucepan. Bring to a boil quickly. Reduce heat to medium and boil 3 or 4 minutes, or until a little dropped into cold water forms a soft ball (234°F). Remove from heat; stir in rolled oats, nuts and vanilla. Drop by teaspoonfuls onto waxed paper; let stand until hardened. Store in refrigerator, if desired. Makes 3 dozen cookies.

Chocolate Mint Meringues
        Lighter Chocolate Desserts - Hershey's
3 egg whites
3/4 teaspoon vanilla
3/4 cup sugar
1/4 cup Hershey's Cocoa
Chocolate Mint Glaze

        Beat egg whites and vanilla until soft peaks form in large mixer bowl. Gradually add sugar, beating until stiff peaks form (tips stand straight). Sift about half of cocoa over egg whites; gently fold until just combined. Repeat with remaining cocoa. Spoon mixture into a pastry bag fitted with large star tip; pipe onto a cookie sheet covered with brown paper. Bake in 300° oven for 35 to 45 minutes or until dry. Peel off paper, cool on wire rack. Prepare Chocolate Mint Glaze. Dip one half of each cookie into glaze; place on a waxed paper-lined cookie sheet until chocolate sets (refrigerate, if needed). About 3 dozen cookies.

Chocolate Mint Glaze: In top of double boiler, melt 1/2 cup Hershey's Semi-Sweet Chocolate Chips and 2 teaspoons shortening. Add 2 to 3 drops mint extract, if desired.

Soyamel® Carob Nut Cookies
  Soyamel® Facts and Recipes
2 cups sifted flour
2/3 cup carob powder or cocoa
1-1/2 teaspoons baking powder
1/2 teaspoon salt
6 tablespoons milk-free margarine
1-1/2 cups brown sugar
1 egg
3/4 cup reconstituted Soyamel®
1/2 teaspoon vanilla
1 cup pecans, chopped

  Combine flour, carob powder or cocoa, baking powder and salt, and sift three times. Melt margarine over hot water. Cool. Add sugar and mix well. Add egg and beat. Add flour mixture alternately with Soyamel®, stirring until blended. Add nuts and vanilla. Drop by teaspoons on oiled cookie sheet; bake at 375°F. about 15 minutes. Yields 3 dozen.

DESSERTS

  Many desserts in the standard cookbooks contain milk, especially ice cream, custards, and sherbets. Several variations are included here to provide some choices in milk substitutes to be used. In most cases, the milk substitutes are interchangeable; for example, Lactaid® can be used in place of Isocal®, etc. The desserts which contain milk substitutes can be a nutritious addition to the lactose-restricted diet. In standard cookbooks, there are many recipes which contain no lactose, such as fruit pies, cobblers, poached and baked fruit desserts, etc.

Apricot Freeze
Soyamel® Facts and Recipes
1 can sweetened peeled apricots (29 oz.) with syrup
1 cup Soyamel® powder
1/4 cup vegetable oil
3 tablespoons lemon juice
1/4 teaspoon salt
1/4 cup water

Liquify or sieve apricots; blend in Soyamel® powder. Slowly beat in oil; add lemon juice and salt. Freeze in hand freezer or in refrigerator trays. If frozen in refrigerator trays, beat several times after mix begins to freeze around edges of tray. Yields approximately 1 quart.

Baked Custard
2 eggs
1/3 cup sugar
1/4 teaspoon salt
2 cups milk substitute

Heat oven to 350°. Beat eggs, sugar and salt slightly to mix. Stir in milk substitute. Pour into 6 custard cups or a 1-1/2 quart baking dish and set in pan of hot water (1" deep). Sprinkle a little nutmeg over tops. Bake 45-50 minutes, or just until a silver knife inserted 1" from edge comes out clean. Chill and serve. Makes 4-5 servings.

Chocolate Covered Bananas

Recipe courtesy of Hershey's Kitchens

2 medium bananas
4 wooden skewers
1 cup Hershey's Mini Chips Semi-Sweet Chocolate
2 tablespoon shortening (*not* butter, margarine or oil)

Peel bananas; cut in half. Insert skewer into each banana half; place on wax paper-covered tray. Cover; freeze until firm. Melt Hershey's Mini Chips Semi-Sweet Chocolate and shortening in top of double boiler over hot water. Remove bananas from freezer just before dipping. Dip each piece into warm chocolate, covering completely. Allow excess to drip off. Cover; return to freezer. Serve frozen. 4 servings.

Cranberry Delight

Soyamel® Facts and Recipes

6 ounces raspberry flavored gelatin (one large package)
2-1/2 cups hot water
1 can crushed pineapple (15 oz.)
1 can whole cranberry sauce (16 oz.)
1 cup chopped celery
1/2 cup chopped pecans
1 cup Special Sour Kreem (see recipe in Sauce Section)

Dissolve gelatin in hot water. Add all remaining ingredients except Special Sour Kreem. Refrigerate. When mixture begins to gel, fold in Special Sour Kreem. Pour into a rectangular dish 7 x 11 x 2 inches or an approximate mold. Yields 7-1/2 cups.

Easy Chocolate Frozen Yogurt
        Recipe courtesy of Hershey's Kitchens
1/4 cup Hershey's cocoa
1/4 cup sugar
2 containers (8 ounces each) vanilla yogurt
1/4 cup light corn syrup
        Combine Hershey's cocoa and sugar in small bowl; set aside. Combine yogurt, corn syrup and cocoa mixture until well blended and smooth in medium mixing bowl; pour into foil-lined loaf pan (9 x 5 x 2-3/4 inches). Cover; freeze several hours or overnight until firm. Spoon into large mixer bowl. With mixer at low speed, beat until smooth but not melted. Return to loaf pan or pour into 1-pint freezer container. Cover; freeze several hours or overnight until firm. Before serving, allow to stand 10 minutes at room temperature. About 1 pint or 4 servings.

Isocal® Custard
        Mead Johnson
3/4 cup Isocal®
1 large egg
5 teaspoons sugar
1/8 teaspoon vanilla
pinch of salt
        Beat egg with salt and sugar in small bowl. Add 1/2 cup of Isocal® cold, plus 1/4 cup Isocal® heated to boiling point. Pour into two custard cups and cover with wax paper. Place in deep pan and pour hot water around cups to level of custard. Bring water to full rolling boil, put lid on pan, turn off heat and let stand for 20 minutes. Chill and serve. Makes 2 servings.
        Variation: Sprinkle with nutmeg.

Isocal® and Fruit Dessert

Mead Johnson

2 cups Isocal®

1 envelope unflavored gelatin

Flavor to taste with fruits, extracts or sweeteners

Sprinkle gelatin into 1/4 cup of Isocal® in small sauce pan. Place over low heat stirring constantly until gelatin dissolves. Remove from heat and add remaining Isocal®. Flavor to taste. Pour into four 1/2 cup serving dishes and chill. Makes 4 servings.

Variation: Chiffon-type gelatin desserts may be prepared by whipping chilled gelatin mixture until light and fluffy. Chill until firm.

Isocal® Raisin-Rice Pudding

Mead Johnson

2 cups Isocal®

1 envelope unflavored gelatin

3/4 cup cooked rice

1/4 cup raisins

1/4 cup sugar

1 teaspoon ground cinnamon

1/2 teaspoon vanilla extract

Sprinkle gelatin into 1/2 cup Isocal® to soften. Heat remaining Isocal® and add to gelatin mixture stirring until gelatin is dissolved. Add cinnamon, sugar and vanilla. Blend well and chill until thickened. Fold in raisins and rice. Spoon into four dessert dishes and chill until firm. Makes 4 servings.

Isocal® Spanish Cream
    Mead Johnson
2 cups Isocal®
1 envelope unflavored gelatin
1/2 cup sugar
2 large eggs, separated
1 teaspoon vanilla extract (or more to taste)
pinch of salt

    Sprinkle gelatin into 1/4 cup Isocal® to soften. Beat egg yolks, sugar and salt in small sauce pan, and gradually stir in remaining 1-3/4 cups Isocal®. Place over low heat stirring constantly until mixture thickens. Add gelatin and stir until dissolved. Beat egg whites until stiff and add with vanilla to gelatin. Blend well, pour into four 1/2 cup dessert dishes and chill. Dessert separates into two layers. Makes 4 servings.

Lemon Ice Cream
    Lacteeze Recipes
3 eggs
1/2 cup sugar
1/2 cup corn syrup
1/4 cup lemon juice
1 teaspoon grated lemon rind
2 cups enzyme-treated milk

    Beat eggs until thick and lemon colored. Gradually add sugar; continue beating until mixture is thick. Add remaining ingredients and blend. Pour into a freezer tray. Freeze until mushy. Turn into a chilled bowl. Beat until fluffy. Freeze. Makes 4 cups.

Microwave Chocolate Pudding

Recipe courtesy of Hershey's Kitchens

1/2 cup sugar

1/4 cup Hershey's Cocoa

3 tablespoons cornstarch

1/4 teaspoon salt

2-1/4 cups enzyme-treated milk (contains 70% less lactose than regular milk)

2 tablespoons butter or milkfree margarine

1 teaspoon vanilla

Combine sugar, cocoa, cornstarch and salt in medium micro-proof bowl; gradually stir in milk. Microwave on high (full power) for 5 minutes, stirring twice during cooking time. Microwave on high 2 to 3 minutes or until mixture thickens. Stir in butter or margarine and vanilla. Pour into dessert dishes; press plastic wrap onto surface. Cool; chill thoroughly. Garnish as desired. 5 servings.

Mixed Fruit Brulee

Soyamel® Facts and Recipes

2 cartons frozen mixed fruit (12 oz. each)

1-1/2 cups Special Sour Kreem (see recipe in Sauce Section)

1/2 cup light brown sugar

Thaw mixed fruit and drain thoroughly. Place in 1-1/2 quart casserole. Spread Special Sour Kreem over fruit. Cover completely. Sprinkle light brown sugar over Sour Kreem layer. Place under broiler until sugar melts. Watch closely to avoid burning. Serve immediately or refrigerate several hours and serve. Serves 4.

Orange Sherbet
2 cups Coffee Rich®
1/2 cup sugar
1/4 cup frozen orange juice concentrate, thawed
1 tablespoon lemon juice
1 teaspoon vanilla extract
        Chill 6 sherbet dishes. In bowl combine all
ingredients. Freeze, stirring often until ice crystals form
throughout and mixture is firm. If mixture becomes solid,
allow to soften in refrigerator for about 20 minutes before
serving. Divide evenly into chilled dishes. Makes 6 servings.

Pumpkin Pie
        Soyamel® Facts and Recipes
1 can pumpkin (29 oz. can or 3-1/2 cups)
1-1/2 cups sugar
2 teaspoons cinnamon
2 teaspoons nutmeg
1/2 teaspoon ginger
1-1/4 cups Soyamel® powder, plus water to make 2 cups
        of liquid
4 eggs, slightly beaten
1/2 teaspoon salt
2-9" pie shells, unbaked
        Combine all ingredients. Mix until smooth. Pour into
unbaked pie shells. Bake at 375°F. for 40 minutes. Cool and
refrigerate.

Strawberry Banana Sherbet

Lacteeze Recipes

1 teaspoon unflavored gelatin
1 tablespoon water
1 cup pureed strawberries
1/2 cup sugar
1/4 cup lemon juice
1 teaspoon grated lemon rind
1 banana, mashed
2 cups enzyme-treated milk

Soften gelatin in water, combine with strawberries and sugar in a small pan and stir over low heat until gelatin and sugar are dissolved. Add lemon juice, rind and banana. Stir mixure into cold enzyme-treated milk. Pour into a metal tray, cover with foil and freeze until firm (2-3 hours). Whirl frozen mixture in a blender or food processor until smooth. Scoop into serving dishes and serve at once. Makes 4 cups. Can be packed into a container, covered and frozen again.

Strawberry Gelatin Dessert

Mead Johnson

1 cup Isocal®
1 small package (3 oz.) strawberry gelatin dessert powder
1/2 cup boiling water
1/2 cup fresh strawberries

Dissolve gelatin in boiling water. Chill until slightly thickened. Pour into blender and add Isocal®. Blend at low speed. Pour into four individual serving dishes. Stir in 1/2 of strawberries, garnish with remainder. Chill and serve. Makes 4 servings.

Strawberry Ice   Requires an ice cream maker
3 one-pound packages sliced frozen strawberries
2 packages unflavored gelatin
1 cup basic sugar syrup - see recipe below.
2 egg whites

Let strawberries stand at room temperature until partially thawed. Soften gelatin in 1/2 cup of cold water, then dissolve in hot sugar syrup. Place 1/3 of the strawberries and 1/3 of the syrup in blender container, then process until pureed. Pour into a large mixing bowl. Repeat blending process two more times with remaining strawberries and syrup. Pour half the strawberry mixture into ice cream maker container. Beat egg whites until soft peaks form, then turn into freezer container. Add remaining strawberry mixture. Freeze according to instructions in ice cream maker. Makes 1/2 gallon.

Basic Sugar Syrup
3/4 cup water
1 cup plus 1 tablespoon sugar

Place water and sugar in large pot over low heat. Heat until sugar is dissolved. Raise to a slow rolling boil then reduce temperature and simmer for 3 minutes. Chill, bottle, and store in refrigerator. Makes approximately 1 cup.

Soyamel® Ice Kreem
Soyamel® Facts and Recipes
1-1/2 cups water
1 cup Soyamel® powder
1/2 cup sugar or 1/3 cup honey
1/2 cup corn oil
1 teaspoon vanilla
Water to make 1 quart of liquid

Blend Soyamel® and water in blender or liquifier. Add other ingredients. Freeze in agitator-type freezer so Kreem is stirred or whipped while freezing. Freeze as hard as possible. This prevents iciness as it sets up.

Variation: For Fruit Ice Kreem use only one cup water to blend Soyamel® powder. Add oil and sugar, then enough sweetened juice or pulp to make one quart and blend well. One cup of sweetened fruit without the juice may be added just before freezing.

Sustacal® Ice
Mead Johnson
1 12-ounce Vanilla Sustacal® Liquid
1/4 teaspoon vanilla extract

Mix Sustacal® Liquid and vanilla extract. Put in freezer tray; and put in freezer until slightly frozen, about 1-1/2 hours. Put into dessert dishes and serve. Makes approximately 1-1/2 cups (2 servings).

Vanilla Ice Cream
        Cooking with Isomil®
1 tablespoon unflavored gelatin
2 tablespoons cold water
1/4 cup granulated sugar
1 13-oz. can Isomil® concentrated liquid (do not use Ready-to-
        Feed)
2 tablespoons clear light corn syrup
2-1/2 tablespoons vegetable oil
2 teaspoons vanilla extract

        Soften gelatin in cold water in a saucepan. Add sugar
and heat slowly to dissolve gelatin and sugar. Cool mixture.
Add remaining ingredients. Blend in a 5 cup or more capacity
blender until thick and creamy. Pour into ice cube tray or loaf
pan or container for use in an electric ice cream maker. (From
this point on, follow instructions that came with your electric
ice cream freezer.) If using the refrigerator, freeze until icy.
Return mixture to blender and blend until smooth. Return to
freezer. Allow to soften slightly before serving.

        Variations: Honey,   brown   sugar,   cinnamon,
strawberries, raspberries and blueberries may be used for
flavoring the ice cream. For fruit flavor, add frozen drained
strawberries or raspberries or fresh fruit such as bananas or
peaches before freezing.

Vitamite® Soft Cream Ice Cream

DSI, Inc.

1 cup Vitamite®
3/4 cup sugar
Flavoring
Color
Fresh fruit (if desired)
30 ice cubes

Pour 1 cup Vitamite® into a blender and add, slowly, while blender is operating at high speed, for full cycle...Sugar, Flavor, Color, Fruit, and 15 ice cubes.

Blend all this together at high speed at a full cycle, and then reblend on full cycle again, but this time add the balance of 15 ice cubes into the blender, feeding them in one at a time, until the mixture becomes thick and creamy.

After mixture thickens, pour desired servings into ice cream dishes or whatever you want to use. Be sure to take out any ice cube lumps that might not have ground up in the final process.

If desired, you may pour the mixture into ice cube trays and freeze for use at a later date...but, allow it to thaw to a creamy stage before using for the best flavor.

EGGS

Savory Eggs
1 cup grated natural Cheddar Cheese
2 tablespoons butter
1/2 cup Coffee Rich® or other liquid lactose-free nondairy
    creamer
1 teaspoon prepared mustard
1/2 teaspoon salt
1/4 teaspoon pepper
6 eggs, slightly beaten
    Heat oven to 325°. Sprinkle cheese in square pan,
9x9x1-3/4". Dot with butter. Mix cream substitute, mustard,
salt and pepper; pour half over cheese. Pour eggs over top,
then remaining cream mixture. Bake 25 minutes. Serve at
once. Makes 6 servings.

Scrambled Eggs
2 eggs
2 tablespoons milk substitute or water
salt and pepper
1 tablespoon butter or milk-free margarine
    Break eggs into a bowl. Add milk substitute or water,
salt and pepper. Beat with fork. Heat butter or milk-free
margarine in moderately hot skillet. Pour in egg mixture and
reduce heat to low. (Eggs should be scrambled slowly and
gently.) When mixture starts to set at bottom and sides, lift
cooked portions with a spatula and turn gently to cook all
portions evenly. As soon as eggs are almost cooked through,
but are still moist and glossy, 5-8 minutes, quickly remove to
hot platter and serve at once. Serves 1-2. Double the recipe to
serve 2-3.

Variations: Scrambled Eggs with Herbs--make Scrambled Eggs (above) except add minced fresh herbs (chives, parsley, tarragon, or chervil) to egg mixture.

Scrambled Eggs with Cheese--make Scrambled Eggs (above) except for each egg add 1 tablespoon grated aged natural Cheddar Cheese, 1/4 teaspoon minced onion to egg mixture. Serve with Tomato Sauce if desired (see recipe in Sauce Section).

ENTREES AND SIDE DISHES

Many standard cookbook recipes for main dishes are lactose-free and require no modification. Check through the recipe to determine if any changes are necessary. If margarine is called for, use butter or milk-free margarine. If breading is required, use lactose-free bread crumbs or cracker crumbs. If canned or dried soup is required in a recipe, use only those which are lactose-free; for example, Campbell's Golden Mushroom Soup is lactose-free, but Campbell's Cream of Mushroom Soup contains cream and whey, and is not lactose-free. In most recipes calling for milk or cream, any of the milk substitutes may be used. (Do not use the sweetened milk substitutes, such as Ensure® or Sustacal® in these recipes.) If cheese is used, be sure it is natural aged cheese.

Chicken in White Sauce (Poulet Blanc)
8 chicken breasts, flattened, deboned, cut in 3 pieces each
1/2 cup olive oil
juice of 1 lemon
1/8 teaspoon pepper
1/2 teaspoon garlic salt
        ***
1/4 cup butter
1 teaspoon olive oil
1 bunch green onions, chopped
6 tablespoons flour
1-1/2 cups chicken stock, recipe follows; or (use 1-1/2
        teaspoons chicken bouillon powder and 1-1/2 cups
        water)
1-1/4 cups milk substitute
salt to taste
white pepper to taste
2 drops Tabasco sauce

Mix olive oil, lemon juice, pepper, and garlic salt. Marinate chicken in this mixture for 2-3 hours or overnight. Chicken will absorb most of the liquid and the flavor. Remove chicken from marinade; set marinade aside. Melt butter in skillet with olive oil. Saute chicken 2-1/2 minutes each side. Remove. Saute green onions slowly, til translucent, not brown. Remove skillet from fire; add flour to green onion-butter-oil mixture. Cook on low heat, stirring constantly until mixture becomes bubbly. Do not allow it to brown. Add any remaining marinade, chicken stock, and milk, stirring constantly so flour won't lump. Add salt, white pepper, Tabasco. Simmer. Add chicken to reheat. Serve over rice; garnish with chopped green onion and thin lemon slices.

To make chicken stock, place 1 quart water in pot; add chicken skin and bones, 1/2 teaspoon basil, 2 bay leaves, tops of 2 bunches of green onions. Simmer for 1-2 hours. This makes a delicately flavored stock.

Escalloped Potatoes

Heat oven to 350° (mod.). Arrange 3 to 4 cups thinly sliced or coarsley grated raw potatoes in layers in 1-1/2 quart baking dish. Sprinkle each layer with minced onion (1 tablespoon in all), salt and pepper; dot with butter or milk-free margarine. Add 1-1/4 cups hot milk substitute. Bake uncovered about 1-1/4 hours. Do not use a sweetened milk substitute. Makes 4 servings.

Macaroni and Cheese

4 cups hot boiled macaroni (7 or 8 oz. uncooked)
2 cups cut-up sharp natural Cheddar Cheese
1 teaspoon salt
1/4 teaspoon pepper
2 cups milk substitute
paprika

Heat oven to 350°. Place cooked macaroni, cheese, salt and pepper in alternate layers in buttered oblong baking dish, 11-1/2x7-1/2x1-1/2", ending with a layer of cheese on top. Pour milk substitute over all. Sprinkle with paprika. Bake 35 to 45 minutes, or until golden brown on top. Serve hot from baking dish garnished with parsley sprigs, pimiento strips, or pepper rings. Serves 6 to 8.

Creamy Macaroni and Cheese

Make Macaroni and Cheese (above)--except use 2 cups Medium White Sauce *in place of milk substitute and seasonings.*

To make a Medium White Sauce:

1/4 cup butter

1/4 cup flour

1/2 teaspoon salt

1/4 teaspoon pepper

2 cups milk substitute

Melt butter over low heat in a heavy saucepan. Blend in flour, seasonings. Cook over low heat, stirring until mixture is smooth, bubbly. Remove from heat. Stir in milk substitute. Bring to a boil, stirring constantly. Boil 1 minute. Makes 2 cups.

Mashed Potatoes

Shake drained, cooked potatoes over low heat to dry. Mash with butter or milk-free margarine, salt, pepper, and hot milk substitute (1/2 cup per 8 potatoes). Whip vigorously until light and fluffy. Sprinkle with paprika, minced parsley, or chives. Do not use a sweetened milk substitute.

Meat Loaf

1 lb. ground beef or veal

1 lb. ground lean pork

3 medium slices milk-free bread, torn in pieces, and 1 cup milk substitute (or 1 cup tomato juice)

1 egg, beaten

1/4 cup minced onion

1 1/4 teaspoon salt

1/4 teaspoon each pepper, dry mustard, sage, celery salt, and garlic salt

1 tablespoon Worcestershire sauce

Heat oven to 350° (mod.). Mix all ingredients thoroughly. For better browning, shape into loaf on shallow baking pan. Bake 1-1/2 hours, or until done. Serve hot or cold. For catsup-topped loaf, spread 3 tablespoons catsup on top before baking. 8 servings.

Scalloped Tuna

2 cans (7 oz. each) tuna, in large pieces

2 cups Ritz crackers, or other lactose-free cracker, or potato chips

3 cups Medium White Sauce (see recipe in Sauce Section; triple the ingredients for this recipe)

3/4 cup sliced ripe olives or sautéed mushrooms

Heat oven to 350°F. Arrange ingredients in alternate layers in buttered 1-1/2 quart baking dish. Finish with a sprinkling of the crackers. Bake 35 minutes. Serve hot. 6 servings.

Spinach Cheese Quiche
    Lacteeze Recipes
1 10-ounce package fresh spinach
1 teaspoon salt
1/2 teaspoon pepper
1 clove garlic, minced
1 cup grated Swiss cheese
1 unbaked pie shell

Custard:
1 cup enzyme-treated milk
2 eggs
2 teaspoons all-purpose flour
2 teaspoons butter or milk-free margarine, melted
    Wash spinach and trim off stems. Place in a large saucepan, cover and cook in a small quantity of water over medium heat until tender, approximately 5 minutes. Drain thoroughly and chop finely. Season spinach with salt, pepper and garlic and place in bottom of unbaked pie shell. Sprinkle with grated cheese. For custard filling, combine milk, eggs, flour and butter, and mix well. Pour over spinach and cheese in pie shell. Bake at 375° for 35-40 minutes or until custard is set and golden. Makes 6 servings.

SAUCES

Basic White Sauces
***

Thin White Sauce
For creamed vegetables, soup
1 tablespoon butter or milk-free margarine
1/2 to 1 tablespoon flour
1/4 teaspoon salt
1/8 teaspoon pepper
1 cup milk substitute
***

Medium White Sauce
For creamed and scalloped dishes
2 tablespoons butter or milk-free margarine
2 tablespoons flour
1/4 teaspoon salt
1/8 teaspoon pepper
1 cup milk substitute
***

Thick White Sauce
For croquettes, souffles
1/4 cup butter or milk-free margarine
1/4 cup flour
1/4 teaspoon salt
1/8 teaspoon pepper
1 cup milk substitute

Melt butter or milk-free margarine over low heat in a heavy saucepan. Blend in flour, seasonings. Cook over low heat, stirring until mixture is smooth, bubbly. Remove from heat. Stir in milk substitute. Bring to boil, stirring constantly. Boil 1 minute. Makes 1 cup. Do not use a sweetened milk substitute.

Coney Island Sauce (blender method)   Soyamel®
1/2 cup water
1/2 cup Soyamel® powder
        Blend to a smooth paste.
Add to blender in a smooth steady stream: 1-1/2 cups vegetable
        oil, then add 6 tablespoons lemon juice.
        Blend the following with a spoon:
1 teaspoon salt
1/4 teaspoon celery salt
1/4 teaspoon garlic salt
1 tablespoon soy sauce
1/4 cup onion, chopped
1 can tomato paste (6 oz.)
        Add to blender. This will be quite stiff. Run blender
only long enough to mix well. (If mixer is used, add the oil a
teaspoonful at a time. Increase only during the last half cup.
Add lemon juice a tablespoonful at a time.)

Mushroom Sauce
        Make 1 cup Medium White Sauce, except sauté 1 cup
sliced mushrooms and 1 teaspoon grated onion in the butter 5
minutes before adding flour.

Special Sour Kreem   Soyamel®
3/4 cup water
1/2 cup Soyamel® powder
1/4 teaspoon cinnamon
3/4 cup buttery flavored oil
1/4 cup lemon juice
        Blend water, Soyamel® and cinnamon in blender. Add
oil slowly and then the lemon juice. Mixture will be quite
thick.

Tomato Sauce
2 tablespoons chopped onion
2 tablespoons chopped green pepper
1 tablespoon butter or milk-free margarine, melted
1 can (8 oz.) tomato sauce
Salt and pepper to taste

Saute onion and green pepper in butter or milk-free margarine until onion is transparent. Add tomato sauce, salt and pepper and heat over low heat. Makes 1-1/4 cups

SOUPS

Soup recipes are available which do not contain any milk, such as bean soup with ham, vegetable soup, beef noodle soup, etc. If a cream soup is desired, the milk substitutes can be substituted for the milk or cream. Do not use the sweetened milk substitutes, such as Ensure® or Sustacal®, for soup cookery.

Apple Vichyssoise
        Serve cold for an unusual soup
3 large Delicious apples
2 quarts chicken stock
1 cup Coffee Rich®
salt to taste
sugar to taste
Fresh lemon juice to taste
1/2 apple cut in very fine strips
        Peel and core apples. Cut into small pieces and cook in broth for about 20 minutes, or until tender. Force through sieve or whirl in blender. Cool and chill. Add Coffee Rich® and mix well. Add salt, sugar, and lemon juice. Cut the apple strips at the last moment so they will not discolor. Sprinkle on top of soup and serve at once. Serves 6.

Creamy Mushroom Soup
    Lacteeze Recipes
3 cups thinly sliced mushrooms
1/4 cup chopped onion
2 cups chicken broth
1/4 cup butter or milkfree margarine
1/4 cup flour
1 1/2 teaspoon salt
3 cups enzyme-treated milk
    Combine mushrooms, onion and chicken broth in a medium saucepan. Bring to a boil. Reduce heat, cover and simmer 15 minutes. Melt butter in a large saucepan. Blend in flour and salt. Gradually stir in enzyme-treated milk. Cook over medium heat, stirring constantly until mixture just comes to a boil and thickens. Stir in undrained mushroom mixture. Serve hot. Makes 6 cups.

Potato Soup
1 tablespoon chopped onion
2 tablespoons butter or milk-free margarine
1 teaspoon salt
1/4 teaspoon celery salt
1/8 teaspoon pepper
1 cup mashed potatoes or boiled potatoes, put through a coarse sieve
2 cups hot milk substitute
    Saute onion in butter. Add seasonings and potatoes; stir in milk substitute. Simmer slowly for about 5 minutes, stirring occasionally. 6 servings.

Yogurt Cucumber Soup
     Serve cold
2 medium cucumbers
1/2 garlic clove, minced
1/2 teaspoon salt
2 cups plus 2 tablespoons plain unflavored yogurt
1/2 cup milk substitute
1-1/2 teaspoon chopped fresh dill or 1/2 teaspoon dill weed
Freshly ground pepper to taste
     Chill a soup tureen.   Pare, seed, and dice 1-1/2 cucumbers.   Score and cut the remaining half cucumber into four equal slices and set aside. In medium bowl combine garlic and salt to make a paste. Add yogurt and milk substitute. Stir to combine. Stir in diced cucumbers and dill, and refrigerate until chilled. Transfer to chilled tureen. Sprinkle with pepper and garnish with reserved cucumber slices. Serve in chilled bowls.   Makes 4 servings. Do not use a sweetened milk substitute.

9

LACTOSE-FREE
FOOD PRODUCTS

Lactose-intolerant individuals should periodically check for lactose on the labels of packaged foods to be purchased. Any change in ingredients will always be shown on the food label, which contains the most accurate and current information about a particular product.

The following pages contain a listing of lactose-free food products from more than forty major food manufacturers. The cooperation and efforts of these companies are appreciated. The products listed here are prepared without lactose, whey, or milk in any form, as of March, 1987. Since product formulations are subject to change, the reader may wish to obtain updated food ingredient lists from time to time. Addresses for each company are provided.

ARMOUR FOOD COMPANIES
Armour Prepared Foods
   Dinner Classics
         Beef Burgundy
         Teriyaki Steak
         Stuffed Green Peppers
         Sweet & Sour Pork
         Cod Almondine
         Boneless Short Ribs with BBQ Sauce
         Chicken Teriyaki
         Sweet & Sour Chicken

Classic Lites
>Sliced Beef with Broccoli
>Beef Pepper Steak
>Veal Pepper Steak

For an update on lactose data, write:
>Armour Frozen Food Company
>Consumer Affairs Department
>P.O. Box 31815
>St. Louis, MO 63131-0815

ARMOUR PROCESSED MEAT COMPANY
Golden Star Ham by Armour
Armour Star Ham (pear shaped)
Armour Star Ham (oblong)
Armour Star Chopped Ham
Armour Star Chopped Pork
Armour Star Spiced Luncheon Meat
Armour Pork Shoulder Picnic
Decker Quality Canned Ham
Quality Luncheon Meat
Quality Chopped Ham
Quality Chopped Pork
Armour Star Corned Beef Brisket
Armour Star Corned Beef Round
Armour Star Bacon
Armour Star Pan Size Bacon
Armour Star Thick Sliced Bacon
Korn Kist Bacon
Tall Corn Bacon
Armour Star Cured Salt Pork
Armour Star Cured Fat Back
Armour Star Fully Cooked Ham, Bone-In
Armour Star Parti Style Ham
Armour Star Parti Style Nugget Ham
Armour Star Speedy-Cut Boneless Ham
Armour Star Speedy-Cut Boneless Nugget Ham
Armour Star Ham Slices
Armour's 1877 Ham
Armour Star Smoked Picnic

Armour Star Country Brand Ham
Armour Star Country Brand Ham, Center and End Slices
Armour Star Melosweet Boneless Ham
Armour Star Semi-Boneless Ham
Armour Star Smoked Fully Cooked Canadian Style Bacon
Armour Star Delite
Armour Star Center Cut Smoked Pork Loin
Armour's 1877 Smoked Fully Cooked Canadian Style Bacon
Armour's 1877 Delite
Campfire Smoked Fully Cooked Canadian Style Bacon
Armour Star German Bologna
Armour Star Cooked Ham
Armour Star Cooked Pork Shoulder Picnic
Armour Star Cooked Salami
Armour Star Cotto Salami
Armour Star Ham-ett
Armour Star Pork Sausage, Mild
Armour Star Pork Sausage, Hot
Armour Star Little Links
Armour Star Tas-T-Links
Armour Star Smokees
Armour Star Bologna
Armour Star Beef Bologna
Armour Star Thick Sliced Bologna
Armour Star Garlic Bologna
Armour Star New England Brand Sausage
Armour Star Pressed Ham
Armour Star Souse
Armour Star Thuringer Summer Sausage
Armour Star German Brand Sausage
Armour Star Kulbassy
Armour Star La Stella Beef Sausage
Armour Star Polish Sausage
Armour Star Smoked Sausage
Armour Star Ring Bologna
Armour Star Ring German Bologna
Armour Star Ring Polish Bologna
Armour Star Genoa Salami
Armour Star Hard Salami
Armour Star Caserta Brand Peperoni
Armour Star Hot Dogs

Armour Star Beef Dinner Franks
Armour Star Dinner Franks
Armour Star Grill Dogs
Armour Star Beef Franks
Armour Star Coarse Ground Grill Dogs
Armour's Old Fashioned Cervelat
Armour's Turkey Franks
Armour Turkey Bologna
Armour Beef Smoked Sausage
Armour Hot Links
Armour Beef Kulbassy
Armour Sliced Pork Loin
Armour Breakfast Ham
Armour Knackwurst
Armerican Brand Summer Sausage
Summer Sausage with Caraway Seeds - Swedish Brand
German Brand Summer Sausage for Beef
Armour's 1877 Old Fashioned Summer Sausage
Armour's 1877 Old Fashioned Beef Summer Sausage
Italian Brand Hard Salami
Italian Brand Peperoni
Armour's Beef Kulbassy
Star Spiced Lunch Meat
Armour Lower Salt Bacon
Armour Lower Salt Hot Dogs
Armour Lower Salt Beef Hot Dogs
Armour Lower Salt Bologna
Armour Lower Salt Beef Bologna
Armour Lower Salt Cooked Salami

For an update on lactose data, write:
Armour Food Companies
Consumer Relations
15101 North Scottsdale Road
Scottsdale, AZ 85254
Telephone: 602 998-6347

BEATRICE/HUNT-WESSON, INC

TOMATO PRODUCTS
- Hunt's® Italian Tomatoes
- Hunt's® Ketchup
- Hunt's® Stewed Tomatoes
- Hunt's® Whole Tomatoes
- Hunt's® Tomato Juice
- Hunt's® Tomato Paste
- Hunt's® Tomato Sauce
- Hunt's® Tomato Sauce with Bits
- Hunt's® Tomato Sauce with Mushrooms
- Hunt's® Tomato Sauce with Onions
- Hunt's® Tomato Sauce Special
- Hunt's® No Salt Added Tomato Juice
- Hunt's® No Salt Added Ketchup
- Hunt's® No Salt Added Tomato Paste
- Hunt's® No Salt Added Tomato Sauce
- Hunt's® No Salt Added Spaghetti Sauce
- Hunt's® No Salt Added Stewed Tomatoes
- Hunt's® No Salt Added Whole Tomatoes
- Hunt's® Meatloaf Fixin's® Tomato Sauce

BEAN PRODUCTS
- Hunt's® Big John's® Beans 'n Fixin's®
- Hunt's® Chili Beans
- Hunt's® Pork & Beans
- Hunt's® Red Kidney Beans
- Hunt's® Small Red Beans

PEANUT BUTTER PRODUCTS
- Peter Pan® Crunchy Peanut Butter
- Peter Pan® Creamy Peanut Butter
- Peter Pan® Salt Free, No Sugar Added Peanut Butter
  (Creamy & Crunchy)
- Peter Pan® Sodium Free Creamy Peanut Butter

FRUITS
- Hunt's® Apricots
- Hunt's® Fruit Cocktail
- Hunt's® Peaches
- Hunt's® Pears

PUDDING PRODUCTS
> Hunt's® Snack Pack® Lemon Pudding
> Hunt's® Snack Pack® Peaches
> Hunt's® Snack Pack® Fruit Cup

OIL & SHORTENING PRODUCTS
> Snowdrift® Shortening
> Wesson® Vegetable Oil
> Wesson® Buttery Flavor Oil
> Wesson® Sunflower Oil
> Wesson® Corn Oil

SLOPPY JOE PRODUCTS
> Hunt's® Original Manwich®

BARBECUE SAUCE PRODUCTS
> Hunt's® Original
> Hunt's® Hickory
> Hunt's® Hot & Zesty
> Hunt's® Onion Flavor
> Hunt's® Southern Style
> Hunt's® Country Style

POPCORN PRODUCTS
> Orville Redenbacher's® Gourmet® Popping Corns
> Orville Redenbacher's® Gourmet® Butter Flavor and Natural
>   Flavor Microwave Popping Corns
> Orville Redenbacher's® Gourmet® Salt Free Butter Flavor and
>   Natural Flavor Microwave Popping Corns

MEXICAN PRODUCTS
> Rosarita® Refried Beans
> Rosarita® Spicy Refried Beans
> Rosarita® Refried Beans with Green Chiles
> Rosarita® Vegetarian Refried Beans
> Rosarita® Pinto Beans
> Rosarita® Mild Taco Sauce
> Rosarita® Hot Taco Sauce
> Rosarita® Picante Salsa
> Rosarita® Mild Chunky Salsa
> Rosarita® Hot Chunky Taco Salsa

Rosarita® Mild Chunky Taco Salsa
Rosarita® Medium Chunky Salsa
Rosarita® Hot Chunky Salsa
Rosarita® Diced Green Chilies
Rosarita® Whole Green Chilies
Rosarita® Jalapeno Nacho Slices
Rosarita® Whole Jalapenos
Rosarita® Tostado Shells
Rosarita® Taco Shells
Rosarita® Corn Tortillas

ORIENTAL PRODUCTS

Frozen

LaChoy® Meat&Shrimp Egg Rolls (30 & 15 count)
LaChoy® Chicken Egg Rolls (15 count)
LaChoy® Shrimp Egg Rolls (15 count)
LaChoy® Lobster Egg Rolls (15 count)
LaChoy® Shrimp Chow Mein Dinner
LaChoy® Shrimp Chow Mein
LaChoy® Chicken Chow Mein Dinner
LaChoy® Chicken Chow Mein
LaChoy® Beef Pepper Oriental Dinner
LaChoy® Beef Pepper Oriental
LaChoy® Sweet & Sour Pork
LaChoy® Sweet & Sour Chicken
LaChoy® Fried Rice with Meat
LaChoy® Chicken Won Ton Soup
LaChoy® Chinese Pea Pods

Canned

LaChoy® Chow Mein Noodles
LaChoy® Rice Noodles
LaChoy® Ramen Noodles - Chicken
LaChoy® Ramen Noodles - Oriental
LaChoy® Ramen Noodles - Beef
LaChoy® Fancy Mixed Chinese Vegetables
LaChoy® Bamboo Shoots
LaChoy® Water Chestnuts
LaChoy® Fried Rice
LaChoy® Bean Sprouts

LaChoy® Chop Suey Vegetables
LaChoy® Shrimp Chow Mein
LaChoy® Pork Chow Mein
LaChoy® Beef Chow Mein
LaChoy® Chicken Chow Mein
LaChoy® Meatless Chow Mein
LaChoy® Vegetable Chow Mein
LaChoy® Beef Pepper Oriental
LaChoy® Sukiyaki
LaChoy® Sukiyaki Skillet Dinner
LaChoy® Sweet & Sour Oriental with Pork
LaChoy® Sweet & Sour Oriental with Chicken
LaChoy® Egg Foo Yung Skillet Dinner
LaChoy® Sweet & Sour Skillet Dinner
LaChoy® Pepper Steak Skillet Dinner

Nut Products
Fisher® Almonds, Natural
Fisher® Almonds, Blanched Slivered
Fisher® Almonds, Dry Roasted, Salted
Fisher® Almonds, Oil Roasted, Salted
Fisher® Cashews, Dry Roasted, Salted
Fisher® Cashews, Oil Roasted, Salted
Fisher® Cashews, Oil Roasted, Lightly Salted
Fisher® Fancy Mixed Nuts, Oil Roasted, Salted
Fisher® Mixed Nuts with Peanuts, Oil Roasted, Salted
Fisher® Mixed Nuts with Peanuts, Oil Roasted, Lightly Salted
Fisher® Cashews and Almonds, Oil Roasted, Lightly Salted
Fisher® Honey Roasted Peanuts
Fisher® Honey Roasted Cashews
Fisher® Honey Roasted Almonds
Fisher® Honey Roasted Pecans
Fisher® Peanuts, Blanched, Dry Roasted, Salted
Fisher® Peanuts, Blanched, Dry Roasted, Lightly Salted
Fisher® Peanuts, Blanched, Dry Roasted, Unsalted
Fisher® Peanuts, Blanched, Oil Roasted, Salted
Fisher® Peanuts, Blanched, Oil Roasted, Lightly Salted
Fisher® Peanuts, In-Shell, Roasted, Salted
Fisher® Peanuts, Spanish, Oil Roasted, Salted
Fisher® Peanuts, Spanish, Oil Roasted, Lightly Salted
Fisher® Pecans, Raw

Fisher® Pistaschios In-Shell, Roasted, Salted
Fisher® Sunflowers In-Shell, Roasted, Salted
Fisher® Sunflowers, Shelled, Dry Roasted, Salted
Fisher® Sunflowers, Shelled, Dry Roasted, Unsalted
Fisher® Sunflowers, Shelled, Oil Roasted, Salted
Fisher® Black Walnuts, Raw
Fisher® English Walnuts, Raw

For an update on lactose data, write:
    Consumer Services
    Beatrice/Hunt-Wesson, Inc.
    P.O. Box 4800
    Fullerton, CA 92634-4800

BEST FOODS
Argo and Kingsford's Cornstarch
Golden Griddle syrup
Hellmann's and Best Foods real mayonnaise
Hellmann's and Best Foods sandwich spred
Hellmann's and Best Foods tartar sauce
Karo dark corn syrup
    light corn syrup
    pancake and waffle syrup
Mazola corn oil
Mazola diet reduced calorie margarine
    unsalted margarine
Mueller's egg noodles
    macaroni
    spaghetti
    all other pasta products
Nucoa margarine
    soft margarine
Skippy creamy peanut butter
    super chunk peanut butter

For an update on lactose data, write:
    Best Foods,CPC International Inc.
    Box 8000
    Englewood Cliffs, NJ 07632

BASKIN-ROBBINS ICE CREAM

Sherbets contain a small amount of milk solids; ices contain no milk products or lactose.

Ices currently listed are: Daiquiri Ice
                                  Pineapple Ice

Sorbets currently listed are: Boysenberry
                                  Red Raspberry

For an update on lactose content, write:
                      Baskin-Robbins Ice Cream
                      31 Baskin-Robbins Place
                      P.O.Box 1200
                      Glendale, CA 91209

BURGER KING®

                      Buns, Whopper, Burger, & Specialty
                      Whopper Patty, Burger Patty
                      Ham
                      Sausage
                      Bacon
                      Ketchup, Mustard
                      Mayonnaise
                      Tartar Sauce
                      Barbecue Sauce
                      Horseradish Sauce
                      Sweet & Sour Sauce
                      French Fries
                      Hash Browns
                      Thousand Island Salad Dressing
                      Reduced Calorie Italian Dressing
                      Apple Pie

For an update on lactose data, write:
                      Burger King Corporation
                      Consumer Relations, Mail Station 1490
                      P.O. Box 520783, General Mail Facility
                      Miami, FL 33152
                      (305) 596-7320

CAMPBELL SOUP COMPANY

CAMPBELL'S SOUPS (condensed)

>Beef Broth
>Beef Broth and Noodles
>Beef Teriyaki
>Beefy Mushroom
>Chicken Barley
>Chicken Broth
>Chicken Broth and Noodles
>Chicken Broth and Rice
>Chicken Broth and Vegetable
>Chicken Gumbo
>Chicken Noodle
>Chicken NoodleO's
>Chicken with Rice
>Chicken & Stars
>Consomme
>Curly Noodles with Chicken
>Golden Mushroom
>Noodles & Ground Beef
>Scotch Broth
>Spanish Style Vegetable (Gazpacho)
>Won Ton

CAMPBELL'S CHUNKY SOUPS

>Chunky Chicken
>Chunky Chicken with Rice
>Chunky Steak & Potato

CAMPPBELL'S SOUP FOR ONE

>Golden Chicken & Noodles

OTHER CAMPBELL PRODUCTS

>Tomato Juice

PREGO

>Plain Spaghetti Sauce
>Spaghetti Sauce with Mushrooms
>Spaghetti Sauce Flavored with Meat

LOW SODIUM PRODUCTS
>   Chicken Noodle
>   Turkey Noodle
>   Chunky Chicken
>   Chunky Vegetable Beef
>   Chicken with Noodles
>   Chunky Beef with Mushroom
>   Chunky Chicken Vegetable

SWANSON'S CANNED PRODUCTS
>   Chunk Chicken
>   Chunk White Chicken
>   Chunk Thigh Chicken
>   Chunk Style Mixin' Chicken
>   Beef Broth
>   Chicken Broth

FRANCO-AMERICAN CANNED PRODUCTS
>   PizzOs
>   Au Jus Gravy
>   Beef Gravy

SWANSON FROZEN PRODUCTS,
>   FROM CAMPBELL SOUP COMPANY

ENTREES
>   Chicken Nibbles with French Fries
>   Fish 'n' Chips

MAIN COURSE
>   Salisbury Steak with Gravy

FRIED CHICKEN PARTS
>   Breast Portions
>   Fried Chicken - Assorted Pieces
>   Nibbles (wing sections)
>   Thighs & Drumsticks

TAKE-OUT STYLE FRIED CHICKEN
>   Take-Out Style Fried Chicken (Assorted Pieces)
>   Take-Out Style Breast Portions

Take-Out Style Chicken Nibbles (Wing Section)
Take-Out Style Drumsticks
Take-Out Style Thighs

SWANSON'S CANNED ENTREES(Ready to Serve)
Chunks O' Chicken

CAMPBELL'S "BOUNTY BRAND"
Beef Goulash

CAMPBELL'S EFFICIENCY FROZEN FOODS
IQF Chicken Nibbles
IQF Frankfurters
IQF Fried Chicken
Macaroni and Beef in Tomato Sauce
Ocean Fish Almondine
Ocean Fish with Lemon Sauce

For an update on lactose data, write:
Campbell Soup Company
Consumer Nutrition Center
Campbell Place
Camden, NJ 08101

CARNATION
Coffeemate
Fruit and Nut Mixes

The Spreadables (sandwich spreads)
Tuna Salad
Turkey Salad
Chicken Salad
Ham Salad

Contadina
Contadina Tomato Products
Contadina Cookbook Sweet 'n Sour Sauce

Albers Products
White Corn Meal
Yellow Corn Meal
Enriched Quick Grits

For an update on lactose data, write:
> Carnation Research Laboratory
> 8015 Van Nuys Boulevard
> Van Nuys, California 91412

DEL MONTE
BRER RABBIT Molasses

CHUN KING Canned
> Beef Chow Mein
> Chicken Chow Mein
> Pork Chow Mein
> Shrimp Chow Mein
> Beef Pepper Oriental
> Bamboo Shoots
> Bean Sprouts
> Chow Mein Vegetables
> Sliced Water Chestnuts

Chow Mein Noodles
Mustard
Soy Sauce
Sweet and Sour Sauce
Stir Fry Vegetables and Sauce Mix for Chow Mein
Stir Fry Vegetables, Sauce Mix and Seasoning for Egg Foo Yung
Stir Fry Vegetables, Sauce Mix and Seasoning for Pepper Steak
Stir Fry Vegetables, Sauce Mix and Seasoning for Sukiyaki
Stir Fry Sauce Glaze Mix for Sweet and Sour Entree
Stir Fry Rice Mix
CHUN KING Frozen Boil in Bag Entrees
> Chicken Chow Mein
> Beef Pepper Oriental
> Shrimp Chow Mein
> Sweet and Sour Pork
> Fried Rice with Pork

COLLEGE INN
> Beef Broth
> Chicken Broth
> Egg Noodles and Chicken

DAVIS Baking Powder

DEL MONTE

All canned fruits
All canned vegetables
All dried fruits
All juices, juice drinks, and nectars
All Mexican sauces, chiles, refried beans
All pickles
All seafood

HAWAIIAN PUNCH

Ready to Drink
Flavor Crystals
Concentrates

For an update on lactose data, write:
Del Monte Consumer Affairs
P. O. Box 3575
San Francisco, CA 94119

DSI, DIEHL SPECIALTIES, INTERNATIONAL

Vitamite
Top "1" Chocolate Beverage
Top "1" Hot Cocoa Mix
Top "1" Nogg
Top "1" Orange Creme
Top "1" Banana
Top "1" Vanilla
Top "1" Strawberry
Sunfruit Big Apple and Spiced Apple Beverage bases
E'ze Fre'ze, vanilla, chocolate, and strawberry flavors

For an update on lactose data, write:
DSI, Diehl Specialties, International
10800 Ambassador Boulevard
St. Louis, MO 63132-1792
Telephone: 314 994-1010

DIETARY SPECIALTIES, INC.
Makers of gluten-free products

Bread and Crackers
>Wel-Plan® Brown Bread Canned
>Bi-Aglut® Crackerbread
>Wel-Plan® Soya Bran Crackers
>Wel-Plan® Crackers

Cookies
>Wel-Plan® Golden Raisin Cookies
>Wel-Plan® Sweet Cookies
>Wel-Plan® Sweet Cookies - Lincoln
>Wel-Plan® Sweet Cookies - Shortcake
>Wel-Plan® Cream Filled Wafers - Chocolate
>Wel-Plan® Cream Filled Wafers - Vanilla
>Wel-Plan® Raisin Cookies
>Wel-Plan® Custard Cream Cookies
>Wel-Plan® Chocolate Chip Cookies

Pasta
>Aproten® Anellini (Ring Macaroni)
>Aproten® Ditalini (Short Ribbed Macaroni)
>Aproten® Rigatini (Ribbed Macaroni)
>Aproten® Tagliatelle (Flat Noodle)
>Wel-Plan® Macaroni
>Wel-Plan® Short Cut Spaghetti
>Wel-Plan® Spaghetti Rings

Mixes
>Dietary Specialties White Bread Mix
>Wel-Plan® White Bread Mix*
>Wel-Plan® Brown Bread Mix*
>Dietary Specialties White Cake Mix*
>Dietary Specialties Chocolate Cake Mix*
>Dietary Specialties Blueberry Muffin Mix*
>Dietary Specialties Bran Muffin Mix*
>Dietary Specialties Brownie Mix
>Wel-Plan® Flour & Baking Mix

*These products contain a trace of lactose.

For an update on lactose data, write:
>Dietary Specialties, Inc.
>P.O. Box 227
>Rochester, NY 14601
>(716) 263-2787

DOLE PACKAGED FOODS COMPANY
Dole Fruit Sorbet
> Strawberry
> Pineapple
> Peach
> Mandarin
> Raspberry

For an update on lactose data, write:
> Dole Packaged Foods Company
> Post Office Box 7330
> San Francisco, CA 94120-7330
> (415) 788-DOLE

DURKEE FOODS
Durkee Flavors, Extracts, and Colors
All Durkee Ground and Whole Spices
All Durkee Dehydrated Vegetables
All Durkee and Snow Crest Cake Decorations
Durkee Coconut Products
Durkee Maraschino Cherries
Durkee Granadaisa Mandarin Oranges
Famous Sauce
Durkee RedHot! Sauce
Durkee Potato Sticks and French Fried Onions
All Durkee Specialty Fish Products

Please read the ingredient label on seasoning blends and the dry mix line.

For an update on lactose data, write:
> Consumer Affairs Department
> Durkee Famous Foods
> SCM Corporation
> Westlake, OH 44145

ENER-G FOODS, INC.

Makers of special diet products for allergy, low sodium, wheat-free and gluten-free diets.

Ener-G White Rice Bread
Ener-G Brown Rice Bread
Ener-G Xanthan Bread
Ener-G Rice Starch Bread (contains butter)
Ener-G Yeast-free Rice Bread
Ener-G Rice & Fiber Bread
Ener-G White Rice Hamburger Buns
Ener-G Brown Rice Hamburger Buns
Ener-G White Rice Hotdog Buns
Ener-G Date Muffins
Ener-G Rice Pizza Shells
Ener-G Melba Toast
Ener-G Plain Croutons
Ener-G Bread Crumbs
Ener-G Rice Cinnamon Rolls
Ener-G Apple-filled Coffeecake
Ener-G Raspberry-filled Coffeecake
Ener-G Fruitcake
Ener-G Cinnamon Crackers
Ener-G Plain Rice Doughnuts
Ener-G Pumpkin Doughnuts
Ener-G Rice Carob Cookies
Ener-G Rice Chocolate Cookies
Ener-G Dutch Cocoa Cookies
Ener-G Chocolate Sandwich Cookies
Ener-G Date Cookies - No Sugar Added
Ener-G Lemon Shortbread Cookies
Ener-G Lemon Sandwich Cookies
Aglutella Vanilla-filled Wafers
Aglutella Macaroons
Aglutella Orange Cookies
Aglutella Rice Spice Cookies
Aglutella Rice Walnut Cookies
Aglutella Gluten-free, Wheat-free & Low Protein Pasta
      Spaghetti
      Spaghetti Rings
      Macaroni
      Tagliatelle

Aproten Gluten-free, Wheat-free & Low Protein Pasta
  Anellini - Small ribbed macaroni
  Ditalini - Short ribbed macaroni
  Rigatini - Long ribbed macaroni
  Tagliatelle - Long flat spaghetti
DeBoles Gluten-free, Wheat-free Corn Pasta
  Thin Spaghetti
  Ziti
  Shells
  Elbows
  Ribbons
Amsnack Gluten-free, Wheat-free Rice Products
  Plain Rice Chips
  Unsalted Plain Rice Chips
  Almond Rice Chips
  Onion Rice Chips
Hol-Grain Gluten-free, Wheat-free Crackers
  Unsalted Lite Snack Thins
  Salted Lite Snack Thins
Kitanihon Rice Crunch Gluten-free, Wheat-free Crackers
  Plain Rice Crunch Crackers
  Onion & Garlic Rice Crunch Crackers
Med-Diet Gluten-free, Wheat-free Soups
  Instant Tomato Soup
  Instant Cream of Mushroom Soup
Med-Diet Low Sodium, Gluten-free Seasonings
  All-Purpose Seasoning
  All-Purpose Seasoning with Lemon
  Herb Seasoning
  Salad Seasoning
Ener-G Gluten-free & Wheat-free Mixes
  Corn Mix
  Corn Germ Cereal
  Corn Bran
  Potato Mix
  Potato Starch
  Fine Potato Flour
  Rice Mix
  Rice Mix - Low Sodium
  Brown Rice Baking Mix
  White Rice Baking Mix

Brown Rice Flour
White Rice Flour
Sweet Rice Flour
Rice Starch
Rice Polish
Rice Bran
Tapioca Flour
Egg Replacer
Methylcellulose
Xanthan Gum
Ener-G Baking Powder
Ener-G Calcium Chloride
Ener-G Calcium Carbonate
Ener-G Soy-free Shortening
Ener-G Milk Substitutes
Lacto-free Non-Dairy Drink
SoyQuik
NutQuik
Ener-G Wheat-free Products
Barley Mix
Oat Mix
Rice 'N Rye Bread Mix
100% Rye Cereal
Millet
Oat Bran

For an update on lactose data, write to:
Ener-G Foods, Inc.
6901 Fox Avenue South
P.O. Box 24723
Seattle, WA 98124-0723
Telephone: (206) 767-6660

R. T. FRENCH COMPANY
Condiments:
Prepared Mustards - All Varieties
Worcestershire Sauce - All Varieties
Barbecue Sauce - All Varieties

Sauce & Gravy Mixes:
>   Au Jus Gravy Makins
>   Sweet & Sour Sauce Mix
>   Teriyaki Sauce Mix
>   Beef Stew Seasoning
>   Chili-O Seasoning
>   Enchilada Seasoning
>   Ground Beef Seasoning with Onions
>   Hamburger Seasoning
>   Meatloaf Seasoning
>   Seasoning Mix for Sloppy Joes
>   Taco Seasoning
>   Chili-O with Onions

Herb-Ox Products:
>   Bouillon Cubes
>   Instant Broth & Seasoning
>   Instant Broth & Seasoning - Low Sodium

All Individual Spices
All Dehydrated Vegetable Flakes
All Cake Decorators
Lemon Pie Filling
Liquid Food Colors

All Spice Blends Except:
>   Salad Seasoning
>   Lemon Peel
>   Orange Peel
>   Imitation Butter Flavor Salt
>   Lemon & Parsley

All Flavoring Extracts Except:
>   Imitation Butter Flavor

For an update on lactose data, write:
>   The R. T. French Company
>   One Mustard Street
>   P. O. Box 23450
>   Rochester, NY 14692

GALAXY CHEESE COMPANY

FORMAGG® is a cheese substitute developed in cooperation with the American Government Study for the Prevention of Heart and Cardiovascular Disorders. It has 35% fewer calories, more calcium, vitamins and minerals than natural cheese. It is lactose-free, high quality protein, and has no cholesterol. Fat content is 7 grams per ounce of partially hydrogenated soybean oil.

FORMAGG® Mozzarella Flavored Cheese Substitute
FORMAGG® No-Salt Mozzarella Flavored Cheese Substitute
FORMAGG® Cheddar Flavored Cheese Substitute
FORMAGG® No Salt Cheddar Flavored Cheese Substitute
FORMAGG® Grated Parmesan Flavored Cheese Substitute

For an update on lactose data, write:
> Galaxy Cheese Company
> R.D. #3 North Gate Industrial Park
> P.O. Box 5204
> New Castle, PA 16105
> Telephone: (800) 441-9419

GENERAL FOODS

Beverage and Breakfast Foods
> BIRDS EYE AWAKE Frozen Concentrate for Imitation
>   Orange Juice
> BIRDS EYE ORANGE PLUS Frozen Concentrate for
>   Orange Breakfast Beverage
> COUNTRY TIME Drink Mixes
> COUNTRY TIME Frozen Concentrates
> COUNTRY TIME Non-Carbonated Ready to Drink
>   Lemonade Flavor Drink
> KOOL-AID Sugar-Sweetened Soft Drink Mixes
> KOOL-AID Unsweetened Soft Drink Mixes
> POSTUM Grain Beverages
> LOG CABIN Syrups (except LOG CABIN Buttered
>   Syrup)
> POST Brand Cereals (except Fortified Oat Flakes and
>   C.W.Post Hearty Granola Cereals)
> TANG Instant Breakfast Drinks (Orange, Grape and
>   Grapefruit flavors)

Coffee Products

MAXWELL HOUSE, YUBAN, SANKA and BRIM
Coffee, All Ground, Freeze-Dried and Instant
MAXIM Freeze-Dried Coffee
MELLOW ROAST Coffee and Grain Beverages

Dessert Products

BAKER'S GERMAN Sweet Chocolate
BAKER'S Semi-Sweet Chocolate
BAKER'S Unsweetened Chocolate
BAKER'S Coconut (all varieties)
BIRDS EYE Frozen Fruits
CALUMET Baking Powder
CERTO Fruit Pectin
D-ZERTA Low Calorie Gelatin Desserts
JELL-O AMERICANA Rice Pudding
JELL-O AMERICANA Tapioca Puddings
JELL-O Gelatin Desserts
JELL-O Puddings and Pie Fillings (except Milk Chocolate,
Chocolate, Chocolate Fudge, Butterscotch
and all JELL-O Instant Puddings and Pie
Fillings)
MINUTE Tapioca
SURE-JELL Fruit Pectin
SWANS DOWN Cake Flour

Main Meal Products

BIRDS EYE AMERICANA Recipe Vegetables (New
Orleans, Pennsylvania Dutch and San
Francisco Style only)
BIRDS EYE Blue Ribbon Combinations (Broccoli,
Carrots, and Pasta in Lightly Seasoned Sauce
only)
BIRDS EYE Combination Vegetables, only those listed
here:
French Green Beans with Sliced Mushrooms
French Green Beans with Toasted Almonds
Carrots with Brown Sugar Glaze
Green Peas and Pearl Onions
Green Peas with Sliced Mushrooms
Rice and Peas with Mushrooms

"Plain" BIRDS EYE Frozen Vegetables (<u>without</u> sauces or
    seasonings added)
BIRDS EYE International Rice Recipes (<u>except</u> Northern
    Italian Style)
BIRDS EYE International Vegetables
BIRDS EYE Stir-Fry Vegetables (Chinese, Japanase and
    Cantonese Style)
GOOD SEASONS Salad Dressing Mixes (Garlic, Italian,
    Low Calorie Italian, Mild Italian,
    Old Fashion French, Onion and Riviera French
    <u>only</u>)
MINUTE Rice
MINUTE Rice Mixes
OPEN PIT Barbecue Sauces
OVEN FRY Coatings
SHAKE 'N BAKE Seasoned Coating Mixes (<u>except</u> for
    Chicken-Barbecue Style and for Chicken-
    Italian Flavor)

For an update on lactose data, write:
    GENERAL FOODS CONSUMER CENTER
    250 North Street
    White Plains, N.Y.10625

GENERAL MILLS

General Mills sent a lengthy listing of lactose-free foods, including
casserole and dessert mixes, granola bars, cake mixes, and cereals.
General Mills requested: "This information is provided in response to your
inquiry and is not to be used for publication."   The reader may request the
listing directly from General Mills.
    Write to:
    General Mills, Inc.
    General Offices
    Post Office Box 1113
    Minneapolis, MN 55440

HERSHEY'S PRODUCTS

HERSHEY'S CONFECTIONERY PRODUCTS
Special Dark sweet chocolate bar
Y & S Nibs Cherry Licorice Candy
Y & S Twizzlers Chocolate Candy
Y & S Twizzlers Licorice Candy
Y & S Twizzlers Strawberry Candy

HERSHEY'S GROCERY PRODUCTS
Chocolate Flavored Syrup
Cocoa
Instant
Unsweetened Baking Chips

For an update on lactose data, write:
Consumer Relations Department
Hershey Foods Corporation
P.O. Box 815
Hershey, PA 17033-0815

HORMEL

Canned Items
Deviled Ham
Ham Patties
Beans and Bacon
Pork Chow Mein
Deviled SPAM Luncheon Meat
Hot Chili with Beans
Sloppy Joes
DINTY MOORE Hashed Potatoes and Beef
MARY KITCHEN Corned Beef Hash
SPAM Smoke Flavored Luncheon Meat
Chili no Beans
Beans and Wieners
SPAM Luncheon Meat
Chili with Beans
Beans and Ham
DINTY MOORE Corned Beef
DINTY MOORE Beef Stew
MARY KITCHEN Roast Beef Hash

Prepared Sausage
>Meat Wieners
>Smoked Pork Sausage (no link)
>LITTLE SIZZLERS Skinless Pork Sausage
>Kolbase Polish Sausage
>Brown 'N Serve Pork Sausage
>Beef Wieners
>Range Brand WRANGLERS Smoked Franks
>Smokies Smoked Sausage
>Beef WRANGLERS Smoked Franks
>Midget Links Pork Sausage

Smoked Meats
>CURE 81 Ham
>RANGE BRAND Bacon
>CUREMASTER Ham
>Bone-in Ham
>BLACK LABEL Bacon
>Ham Roll

PERMA-FRESH LUNCH MEATS
>Smoked Cooked Ham
>Jellied Beef Loaf
>Peppered Loaf
>Red Peppered Ham
>Corned Beef Loaf
>Cooked Pastrami
>Black Peppered Ham
>Sliced Meat Bologna
>Chopped Ham
>New England Brand Luncheon Meat
>Sliced Beef Bologna

For an update on lactose data, write:
>Geo. A. Hormel & Company
>Supervisor of Consumer Response
>P. O. Box 800
>Austin, MN 55912

KEEBLER COMPANY
Cookies

Animal Crackers
Oatmeal Cremes
Old Fashion Oatmeal
Pecan Sandies
Soft Batch Cookies
French Vanilla Cremes
Puddin' Cremes Butterscotch
Puddin' Cremes Chocolate
Puddin' Cremes Double Chocolate

Crackers

Club Crackers
Export Sodas
Harvest Wheats
Honey Grahams
Sea Toast
Soup & Oyster
Stone Creek Butterthins
Stone Creek Hearty Rye
Stone Creek Sour Dough
Stone Creek Cracked Wheat
Tato Skins Baked Potato
Toasteds Bacon
Toasteds Pumpernickel
Toasteds Rye
Toasteds Sesame
Town House
TUC Crackers
Waldorf Low Sodium
Wheatbury
Zesta Saltines
Zesta Unsalted Tops

Specialties

All cones (Vanilla, Party, Sugar)
All Butter Pretzels (Braids, Knots, Mini-Knots, Nibblers)
All Ready-Crusts (Butter, Chocolate, Graham, Tarts)

For an update on lactose data, write:
>   KEEBLER COMPANY
>   Consumer Relations
>   One Hollow Tree Lane
>   Elmhurst, IL 60126
>   (312) 833-2900

KNOUSE FOODS

Lucky Leaf Pie Filling
>   Apple
>   Old Fashioned Apple
>   Apricot
>   Blackberry
>   Blueberry
>   Cherry
>   Lemon
>   Mincemeat
>   Peach
>   Pineapple
>   Pumpkin
>   Raisin
>   Strawberry
>   Strawberry-Rhubarb
>   Lite Apple
>   Lite Blueberry
>   Lite Cherry

Lucky Leaf Apple Sauce
>   Regular Apple Sauce
>   Natural Apple Sauce
>   Chunky Apple Sauce
>   Unsweetened Apple Sauce
>   Lite Apple Sauce

Lucky Leaf Canned Fruit
>   Sliced Apples
>   Red Tart Pitted Cherries
>   Syrup Pack Blueberries

Lucky Leaf Apple Juice and Cider
> Regular Apple Juice
> Natural Apple Juice
> Old Fashioned Apple Cider
> Sparkling Apple Cider
> Frozen Apple Juice Concentrate
> Frozen Natural Apple Juice Concentrate

Lucky Leaf Apple Butter

Lucky Leaf Specialty Products
> Whole Baked Apples
> Dutch Baked Apples
> Spiced Crab Apples
> Spiced Apple Rings, red
> Spiced Apple Rings, green

Lucky Leaf Vinegar
> Pure Apple Cider Vinegar
> White Distilled Vinegar

Musselman's Pie Filling
> Apple
> Blackberry
> Blueberry
> Cherry
> Lemon
> Peach
> Pineapple
> Strawberry

Musselman's Apple Sauce
> Regular Apple Sauce
> Natural Apple Sauce
> Golden Delicious Apple Sauce
> Homestyle Chunky Apple Sauce
> Unsweetened Apple Sauce

Musselman's Canned Fruits
> Sliced Apples
> Red Tart Pitted Cherries
> Syrup Pack Blueberries

Musselman's Apple Juice and Cider
> Regular Apple Juice
> Natural Apple Juice
> Old Fashioned Apple Cider
> Sparkling Cider
> Frozen Apple Juice Concentrate
> Frozen Natural Apple Juice Concentrate

Musselman's Apple Butter

Musselman's Specialty Products
> Whole Baked Apples
> Dutch Baked Apples
> Spiced Crab Apples
> Spiced Apple Rings, red
> Spiced Apple Rings, green

Musselman's Miscellaneous Juices
> B-C Orange Apricot
> B-C Orange Pineapple
> B-C Apple Grape
> B-C Grapefruit Orange
> B-C Apple Cherry

Musselman's Vinegar
> Pure Apple Cider Vinegar
> White Distilled Vinegar

For an update on lactose data, write:
> Knouse Foods
> Peach Glen, PA 17306
> Telephone: (717) 677-8181

LEGUME

Under 300 calorie entrees
Vegetable Lasagne with tofu & sauce
Cannelloni Florentine with tofu & sauce
Stuffed Shells Provencale with tofu & sauce
Mexican Enchiladas with tofu & sauce
Sesame Ginger Stir-Fry with tofu & brown rice
Sweet & Sour Tofu with whole wheat noodles
Classic Lasagne with tofu & sauce
Classic Manicotti with tofu & sauce
Meatless Pepper-Steak with kofu & noodles
Round Ravioli with tofu

Legume Tofuffins - Raisin/Bran & Blueberry

Legume light Creamy Mousse Pies - Double
Chocolate & Lemon/Orange

Legume Light Mayo-Spread
Legume Light Dressings - Russian Style, Creamy
Italian, Mustard Dill, and French Style

For an update on lactose data, write:
Legume, Inc.
170 Change Bridge Road A4
Montville, NJ 07045
Telephone: 201 882-9190

LOMA LINDA FOODS

Soyalac Ready-to-Serve
Soyalac Powder
Soyalac Concentrate
I-Soyalac Concentrate
I-Soyalac Ready-to-Serve
Soyagen No Sucrose
Soyagen All Purpose

For an update on lactose data, write:
Loma Linda Foods
11503 Pierce Street
Riverside, CA 92515
(714) 687-7800

LONGACRE

Longacre Deli-Slice Brown & Roasted Chicken Breast
Longacre Turkey Salad
Longacre Chicken Salad
Longacre Tuna Salad
Longacre Breaded Turkey Nuggets
Longacre Breaded Chicken Nuggets
Longacre Lean-Lite Deli Turkey Breast
Longacre Lean-Lite Deli Smoked Turkey Breast
Longacre Lean-Lite Deli Turkey Ham
Longacre Sliced Turkey Breast
Longacre Sliced Turkey Ham
Long Valu Institutional White Turkey Roll
Longacre Oven Roasted Turkey Thighs
Longacre Smoked Turkey Breast
Longacre Whole Smoked Turkey
Longacre Turkey Salami
Longacre Turkey Ham and 12% Water Added
Longacre Turkey Ham
Longacre Turkey Pastrami
Longacre Turkey Bologna
Longacre Turkey Franks
Longacre Ground Turkey
Longacre Mild Turkey Sausage
Longacre Hot Turkey Sausage

For an update on lactose data, write:
Horace W. Longacre, Inc.
Franconia, PA 18924-0008
(215) 723-4335

McDONALD'S®

Buns
Hamburger Patty
Big Mac without cheese
French Fries
Soft Drinks

NABISCO BRANDS

Cookies and Crackers

ALMOST HOME Iced Oatmeal Raisin Cookies
BAKERS BONUS Sugar Rings Cookies
BUGS BUNNY Graham Cookies
Chocolate Grahams
Chocolate Snaps
Cocoanut Macaroon Soft Cakes
Fudge Chocolate Chip Cookies
GIGGLES Sandwich Cookies
Old Fashion Ginger Snaps
PANTRY Molasses Cookies
Pecan Shortbread Cookies
Pinwheels Chocolate & Marshmallow Cakes
Cinnamon Treats
Cracker Meal
CROWN PILOT Crackers
DANDY Soup & Oyster Crackers
French Onion Thins Snack Crackers
NABISCO Graham Crackers
NABISCO Graham Cracker Crumbs
HONEY MAID Graham Crackers
MEAL MATES Sesame Bread Wafers
Nutty WHEAT THINS Snack Crackers
OYSTERETTES Soup & Oyster Crackers
Potato 'n Sesame Snack Thins
PREMIUM Crackers Unsalted Tops
PREMIUM Saltine Crackers
RITZ Crackers
SEA ROUNDS Crackers
SOCIABLES Crackers
SULTANA Soda Crackers

TRISCUIT Wafers
TRISCUIT Wafers Low Salt
TRISCUIT Wafers No Salt Added
UNEEDA Biscuits Unsalted Tops
WHEAT THINS Snack Crackers
WHEAT THINS Snack Crackers Low Salt
WHEATSWORTH Stone Ground Wheat Crackers

Dromedary Products and Home Hearth Bread Mixes
DROMEDARY Corn Bread Mix
DROMEDARY Corn Muffin Mix
DROMEDARY Gingerbread Mix
DROMEDARY Pound Cake Mix
DROMEDARY Chopped Dates
DROMEDARY Pitted Dates
DROMEDARY Pimientos
HOME HEARTH French Bread Mix

Cones and Cups
COMET Cones and Cups
Chocolate Flavored COMET Cups
COMET Sugar Cones

Cereals
CREAM OF RICE Cereal
CREAM OF WHEAT Cereal
Instant
Quick
Regular
Mix 'n Eat CREAM OF WHEAT Cereal Baked Apple 'n
Cinnamon
NABISCO Shredded Wheat
SPOON SIZE Shredded Wheat
TOASTED WHEAT AND RAISINS Cereal
NABISCO 100% Bran Cereal
TEAM Flakes

Snack Products
Corn DIGGERS Corn Snacks
MISTER SALTY Dutch Pretzels
MISTER SALTY VERI-THIN Pretzel Sticks

MISTER SALTY Pretzel Sticks
MISTER SALTY Pretzel Logs
MISTER SALTY Pretzel Nuggets
MISTER SALTY Pretzel Mini
MISTER SALTY Pretzel Mini Mix
MISTER SALTY Pretzel Rings
MISTER SALTY Pretzel Rods
MISTER SALTY Pretzel Twists

Planters Snacks

PLANTERS Tortilla Chips, Traditional
PLANTERS Corn Chips
PLANTERS Pretzels

Royal Gelatins

ROYAL Gelatin Dessert Apple
ROYAL Gelatin Dessert Blackberry
ROYAL Gelatin Dessert Cherry
ROYAL Gelatin Dessert Lemon
ROYAL Gelatin Dessert Lemon-Lime
ROYAL Gelatin Dessert Lime
ROYAL Gelatin Dessert Orange
ROYAL Gelatin Dessert Peach
ROYAL Gelatin Dessert Pineapple
ROYAL Gelatin Dessert Raspberry
ROYAL Gelatin Dessert Strawberry
ROYAL Gelatin Dessert Strawberry Banana
ROYAL Gelatin Dessert Tropical Fruit

Royal Sugar Free Gelatins and Puddings

ROYAL Sugar Free Gelatin Dessert Cherry
ROYAL Sugar Free Gelatin Dessert Lime
ROYAL Sugar Free Gelatin Dessert Orange
ROYAL Sugar Free Gelatin Dessert Raspberry
ROYAL Sugar Free Gelatin Dessert Strawberry
ROYAL Sugar Free Instant Pudding Chocolate

Royal Instant Puddings

ROYAL Instant Pudding Banana Cream
ROYAL Instant Pudding Chocolate
ROYAL Instant Pudding Chocolate Chocolate Chip

ROYAL Instant Pudding Chocolate Mint
ROYAL Instant Pudding Dark 'n Sweet
ROYAL Instant Pudding Lemon
ROYAL Instant Pudding Pistachio Nut
ROYAL Instant Pudding Toasted Coconut
ROYAL Instant Pudding Vanilla

Royal Cooked Puddings and No-Bake Mixes
ROYAL Pudding Banana Cream
ROYAL Pudding Chocolate
ROYAL Pudding Custard
ROYAL Pudding Dark 'n Sweet
ROYAL Pudding Flan with Caramel Sauce
ROYAL Pudding Lemon Pie Filling
ROYAL Pudding Vanilla
ROYAL Pudding Vanilla Tapioca

Confections
Welch's CORTINA Dark Chocolate Covered Cherries
CORTINA Thin Mints
JUNIOR MINTS Candy
Peppermint Patties
PINE BROS. Cough Drops Assorted Honey/Wild Cherry

Life Savers Gum Products
BEECH NUT Gum
Cinnamon
Fancy Fruit
Peppermint
Spearmint

BEECHIES Candy Coated Gum
Fruit
Peppermint
Pepsin
Spearmint

BUBBLE YUM Bubble Gum
Bananaberry Split
Cherry
Fruit

    Grape
    Luscious Lime
    Pink Lemonade
    Spearmint
    Strawberry
    Tropical Punch
    Wacky Fruit (Peach-Apricot)

Sugarless BUBBLE YUM Bubble Gum
    Fruit
    Grape
    Orange
    Strawberry

FRUIT STRIPE Gum
    Cherry
    Lemon
    Lime
    Orange

FRUIT STRIPE Bubble Gum
    Cherry
    Fruit
    Grape
    Lemon

REPLAY Gum
    Cinnamon
    Peppermint
    Spearmint

CARE*FREE Sugarless Gum
    Cinnamon
    Fruit
    Peppermint
    Spearmint

CARE*FREE Sugarless Bubble Gum
    Fruit
    Orange
    Strawberry
    Wintergreen

LIFE SAVERS Roll Candy
      Cin-O-Mon
      Cryst-O-Mint
      Fancy Fruits
      Five Flavor
      Pep-O-Mint
      Root Beer
      Spear-O-Mint
      Stik-O-Pep
      Strawberry
      Tangerine
      Tropical Fruits
      Wild Cherry
      Wint-O-Green

BEECH-NUT Cough Drops

Sugar-Free BREATH SAVERS MINTS
      Cinnamon
      Peppermint
      Spearmint
      Wintergreen

LIFE SAVERS Lollipops
      Assorted Flavors
      Carnival Flavors
      Swirled Flavors

LIFE SAVERS Sours

BONKERS! Fruit Candy
      Grape
      Orange
      Strawberry
      Watermelon

CHUCKLES CANDIES
      CHUCKLES Cherry Jellies
      CHUCKLES Family Assortment
      CHUCKLES Fruit Jellies
      CHUCKLES Jelly Beans

CHUCKLES Jelly Candy Bar
CHUCKLES Jelly Eggs
CHUCKLES Jelly Rabbits
CHUCKLES Jelly Rings
CHUCKLES Ju Ju Rabbits
CHUCKLES Ju Jubes
CHUCKLES Licorice Jellies
CHUCKLES Licorice Jelly Eggs
CHUCKLES Marshmallow Eggs - Plain and
    Speckled
CHUCKLES Nougat Centers
CHUCKLES Nougat Eggs
CHUCKLES Orange Slices
CHUCKLES Spearmint Leaves
CHUCKLES Spice Drops
CHUCKLES Spice Strings
CHUCKLES Spice Sticks and Drops
CHUCKLES Wild Fruit Berries
CHUCKLES Cinnamon Softees
CHUCKLES Jelly Bunny Fruit Softees
CHUCKLES Jelly Mint Softees
CHUCKLES JuJu Softees
CHUCKLES Licorice Softees

BLUE BONNET MARGARINE
    Diet BLUE BONNET Margarine

FLEISCHMANN'S MARGARINE
    Diet FLEISCHMANN'S Margarine
    Diet FLEISCHMANN'S Margarine with Lite Salt
    FLEISCHMANN'S Margarine Unsalted Stick
    Sweet Unsalted FLEISCHMANN'S Margarine Pareve

FLEISCHMANN'S YEAST AND EGG BEATERS
    FLEISCHMANN'S Active Dry Yeast - Regular
    FLEISCHMANN'S Yeast - Consumer Compressed
    FLEISCHMANN'S EGG BEATERS Cholesterol-free
        Egg Product

PLANTERS NUTS
            Blanched Slivered Almonds
            Blanched Whole Almonds
            Natural Sliced Almonds
            Natural Whole Almonds
            Pecan Chips
            Pecan Halves
            Pecan Pieces
            Black Walnuts
            English Walnuts
            English Walnut Halves & Pieces
            Fruit 'n Nut Mix
            PLANTERS Dry Roasted Almonds
            PLANTERS Dry Roasted Cashews
            PLANTERS Dry Roasted Unsalted Cashews
            PLANTERS Dry Roasted Cashews Halves
            PLANTERS Dry Roasted Honey Peanuts
            PLANTERS Dry Roasted Mixed Nuts
            PLANTERS Dry Roasted Peanuts
            PLANTERS Unsalted Dry Roasted Peanuts
            PLANTERS Dry Roasted Lite Peanuts
            PLANTERS Dry Roasted Pistachios
            PLANTERS Dry Roasted Sesame Nut Mix
            PLANTERS Dry Roasted Sunflower Kernels
            PLANTERS Dry Roasted Sunflower Nuts
            PLANTERS Dry Roasted Sunflower Nuts - Unsalted
            PLANTERS Honey Roast Cashews
            PLANTERS Honey Roast Cashews and Peanuts
            PLANTERS Honey Roast Peanuts
            PLANTERS Red Pistachios
            PLANTERS Nut Topping
            PLANTERS Oil Roasted Cashew Halves
            PLANTERS Oil Roasted Cashews
            PLANTERS Oil Roasted Cocktail Nuts
            PLANTERS Oil Roasted Cocktail Peanuts
            PLANTERS Oil Roasted Unsalted Cocktail Peanuts
            PLANTERS Oil Roasted Mixed Nuts
            PLANTERS Oil Roasted Deluxe Mixed Nuts
            PLANTERS Oil Roasted Regular Mixed Nuts
            PLANTERS Oil Roasted Unsalted Mixed Nuts
            PLANTERS Oil Roasted Peanuts

PLANTERS Oil Roasted Salted Peanuts
PLANTERS Oil Roasted Redskin Peanuts
PLANTERS Oil Roasted Red Pistachios
PLANTERS Oil Roasted Sesame Nut Mix
PLANTERS Oil Roasted Spanish Peanuts
PLANTERS Oil Roasted Sunflower Kernels
PLANTERS Oil Roasted Sunflower Nuts
PLANTERS Peanut Oil
PLANTERS Popcorn Oil
PLANTERS Raw Spanish Peanuts
PLANTERS Salted Pistachios
PLANTERS Salted Peanuts
PLANTERS Smoked Almonds
PLANTERS Sunflower Seeds
PLANTERS Tavern Nuts
Roasted-in-shell Peanuts
Salted-in-shell Peanuts
PLANTERS Naturally Nut 'n Fruit Bars
    Peanut/Raisin Bar
    Walnut/Apple Bar
    Almond/Apricot Bar
    Almond/Pineapple Bar
PLANTERS Jumbo Block
PLANTERS Peanut Candy

For an update on lactose data, write:
    Consumer Information Center
    Nabisco Brands, Inc.
    East Hanover, NJ 07936
    (201) 898-7100

MLG LABS, INC.

Nurture® Frosty Cal™
Nurture® Apricot Cooler™

For an update on lactose data, write:
    MLG Labs, Inc.
    400 Washington Street
    Braintree, MA 02184
    (617) 849-6109

NUTRI-FOODS INTERNATIONAL INC.
Minute Maid® Fruit Juicee™
> Cherry
> Grape
> Strawberry
> Lemon
> Fruit Punch
> Orange
> Pineapple

For an update on lactose data, write:
> Nutri-Foods
> P.O. Box 2079
> Houston, TX 77252
> (713) 888-5581

ORE-IDA FOODS
> GOLDEN CRINKLES®
> GOLDEN FRIES®
> Shoestrings
> PIXIE CRINKLES®
> COUNTRY STYLE® DINNER FRIES
> Cottage Fries
> Southern Style Hash Browns
> Shredded Hash Browns
> Heinz Deep Fries Regular Cuts
> Heinz Deep Fries Crinkle Cuts
> Heinz Deep Fries Shoestrings
> TATER TOTS®
> TATER TOTS® Onion Flavor
> TATER TOTS® Bacon Flavor
> CRISPY CROWNS!®
> CRISPY CROWNS!®/Onion
> Small Whole Peeled Potatoes
> Stew Vegetables
> O'Brien Vegetables
> ONION RINGERS®
> Chopped Onions
> Cob Corn
> CRISPERS!®

HOME STYLE POTATO PLANKS™
HOME STYLE POTATO THINS
HOME STYLE POTATO WEDGES™
GOLDEN PATTIES®
LITES Crinkle Cuts
LITES French Fries
LITES Steak Fries
LITES Natural Fries
LITES Shoestrings
Microwave Crinkle Cuts
Microwave TATER TOTS®

For an update on lactose data, write:
Consumer Relations
Ore-Ida Foods, Inc.
P. O. Box 10
Boise, Idaho 83707-0010
(208) 383-6100

ORVAL KENT FOOD COMPANY, INC.
SIGNATURE SALADS®
Crabmeat Flavored Salad
Shrimp Salad
Chicken Salad
Tuna Salad
Ham Salad
Egg Salad
Fresh Button Mushroom Salad
Sliced Mushroom Salad
Marinated Artichoke Salad
Antipasto Salad (contains Provolone Cheese)
Meat Tortellini Salad (contains Romano Cheese)
Our Prima Pasta Salad (contains Parmesan
Cheese)
Mexican Shrimp Salad Veracruz
Red Potato & Egg Salad Supreme
Pasta Pesto with Crabmeat Salad (contains Italian
Style Cheese and Parmesan Cheese)
Oriental Chicken Salad
Seafood Salad with Crab & Shrimp
California Medley Salad
Garden Olive Salad

Other Orval Kent Products
    Diced Potato Salad
    Mustard Potato Salad
    German Potato Salad
    Potato and Egg Salad
    Short Shred Slaw
    Chopped Slaw
    V & O Health Slaw
    Macaroni Salad
    Mustard Macaroni Salad
    Tri-Bean Salad
    Cucumber Salad
    Carrot-Raisin Salad
    Barbecue Beans
    Creme Desserts (Confetti, Strawberry)
    Strawberry Fruit Gelatin
    Cranberry Nut Gelatin Salad, seasonal

For an update on lactose data, write:
    Orval Kent Food Company
    120 W. Palatine Road
    Wheeling, IL 60090
    (312) 459-9000

OSCAR MAYER

BACON
Bacon, Regular
Bacon, 1/8" Thick Sliced
Bacon, Center Cut
Bacon Bits

HAM
Ham, Boneless Jubilee
Ham, Jubilee Canned
Ham Slice, Water Added
Ham Steaks, Water Added

LINKS
Beef Franks
Polish Sausage
Ring Bologna, Wisconsin Made
Smokie Links Sausage
Smokies, Beef
Smokies Sausage, Little
Wieners
Wieners, Little

MEAT SPREADS
Braunschweiger Liver Sausage
Braunschweiger, German Brand
Chili Con Carne Concentrate
Ham Salad Spread
Sandwich Spread

SLICED COLD MEATS
Beef, Italian Style
Bologna
Bologna, Beef
Bologna, Garlic Beef
Braunschweiger Liver Sausage
Canadian Style Bacon
Chicken Breast, Smoked
Corned Beef
Corned Beef Loaf, Jellied
Ham, Chopped
Ham, Honey
Ham, Italian Style Ckd.
Ham, Cracked Pepper
Ham, Peppered Chopped
Ham, Smoked Cooked
Head Cheese
Liver Cheese
Luncheon Meat
New England Brand Sausage
Pastrami
Salami, Cotto
Salami, Beef Cotto
Salami, Beef Machiaeh Brand

Salami, Beef Machiaeh Brand
Salami for Beer
Salami for Beer, Beef
Turkey Breast, Smoked

MISCELLANEOUS
Breakfast Strips Beef Lean 'n Tasty
Breakfast Strips Pork Lean 'n Tasty
Sweet Morsel (Pork Shoulder)

PORK SAUSAGE
Little Friers Pork Sausage Links
Pork Sausage Links
Pork Sausage Roll

For an update on lactose data, write:
Oscar Mayer Foods Corporation
P.O. Box 7188
Madison, WI 53707

PILLSBURY PRODUCTS

As of January, 1986, the following brands of products from Pillsbury did not contain milk or milk products. Each time purchases are made, check the ingredient list since formulations do change. An updated list can be requested yearly; send requests to Consumer Response, The Pillsbury Company, Box 550, Minneapolis, MN 55440-0550.

TOTINO'S FOOD PRODUCTS
Microwave Popcorn: Original and Salt Free
PILLSBURY Microwave Buttermilk Pancakes

GREEN GIANT PRODUCTS
All Green Giant Canned Vegetable Products

BAKED ENTREES:
Stuffed Peppers
Stuffed Cabbage
Salisbury Steak

BOIL-IN-BAG (BIB) ENTREES:

TWIN POUCH BIB ENTREES:
    Szechwan Beef
    Chicken w/Garden Vegetables
    Shrimp Creole

SIDE DISHES:
    Rice Pilaf
    Rice Medley
    White & Wild Rice

BOIL-IN-BAG (BIB) VEGETABLES
    Cream Style Corn
    HARVEST FRESH Brand:
        Lima Beans
        Mixed Vegetables
        Sweet Peas
        Cut Green Beans
        Cut Broccoli
        Golden Corn
        Cut Spinach
        Broccoli Spears
        White Corn
        Early June Peas

GREEN GIANT PRODUCTS
    POLYBAG VEGETABLES
        Corn on Cob
        Sweet Peas
        Cut Green Beans
        White Corn
        NIBLETS Corn
        LE SUEUR Early Peas
        Cut Broccoli
        Whole Leaf Spinach
        Brussels Sprouts
        Mixed Vegetables
        Cauliflower Florets
        Broccoli Spears
        Broccoli-Carrot Fanfare
        Broccoli-Cauliflower Supreme
        Corn-Broccoli Bounty
        Sweet Peas-Cauliflower Medley

KOUNTY KIST Brand
    Peas
    Peas & Carrots
    Golden Corn
    Cut Green Beans
    White Corn
    Mixed Vegetables
    Cauliflower
    Brussels Sprouts
    Cut Broccoli

DRY GROCERY PRODUCTS
    Enriched Farina
    Hot Roll Mix
    Pie Crust Mix and Sticks
    Ballard Cornbread Mix
    PILLSBURY'S BEST Instant Dry Yeast
    POPPIN' FRESH Bread Mix - all varieties
    PILLSBURY'S BEST and BALLARD Brand
        Flours - all varieties
    PILLSBURY PLUS Cake Mixes - all flavors
        <u>except</u> Strawberry, Carrot 'n Spice,
        White, and Butter Recipe
    Chocolate Macaroon BUNDT Cake Mix
    Quick Bread Mixes - all flavors <u>except Cherry Nut</u>
        <u>and Blueberry Nut</u>
    Apple Cinnamon Coffee Cake Mix
    Gingerbread Mix, Fudge and Walnut Brownie
        Mixes
    Fluffy White, Coconut Pecan and Coconut Almond
        Frosting Mixes
    Cake & Cookie Decorator Icing - all colors
    READY-TO-SPREAD Frosting Supreme - all
        flavors <u>except</u> Milk Chocolate, Sour Cream, and
        Cream Cheese
    Brown and Home Style Gravy Mixes
    HUNGRY JACK Potato Flakes
    HUNGRY JACK Extra Lights and Blueberry
        Pancake Mixes
    Pillsbury Shelf Stable Microwave Popcorn
    LIQUID SWEET*10 and SPRINKLE SWEET
        Sweeteners

Ultimate Brownie Mixes - all varieties
Idaho Mashed Potatoes*
Idaho Spuds Mashed Potatoes*
Hash Brown Potatoes
Potato Pancake Mix
*Milk recommended in preparation.

REFRIGERATED PRODUCTS
Biscuits:
Ballard Ovenready
Ballard Buttermilk
HUNGRY JACK Fluffy Buttermilk
HUNGRY JACK Flakey Buttermilk
HUNGRY JACK Extra Rich Buttermilk
Pillsbury Extra Lights Flaky Buttermilk
Tenderflake Buttermilk
Tenderflake Baking Powder
Pillsbury Big Country Artificial Buttermilk
Soft Breadsticks
Crusty French Loaf
Spread 'n Bake Fudge Brownies
PIPIN' HOT Loaf - all varieties
Orange Danish, Caramel Danish and Quick Cinnamon
Sweet Rolls
Slice 'n Bake Cookies: Oatmeal, Peanut Butter, Oatmeal
Raisin
PILLSBURY BEST Chocolate Chip, Oatmeal Raisin &
Peanut Butter Cookies
Turnovers - all flavors
Plain Wiener Wraps
All Ready Pie Crust

For an update on lactose data, write:
Consumer Response
The Pillsbury Company
P.O.Box 550
Minneapolis, MN 55440-0550

PROCTER & GAMBLE
Citrus Hill Plus Calcium Orange Juice Beverage
Citrus Hill Plus Calcium Grapefruit Juice Beverage

For an update on lactose data, call:
Procter & Gamble
(800) 358-8707

QUAKER OATS COMPANY
Wolf Brand Chili with Beans
Wolf Brand Texas Two Step Chili Fixins
Wolf Brand Extra Spicy Chili with Beans
Wolf Brand Chili without Beans
Wolf Brand Chili-Mac
Wolf Brand Beef Stew
Wolf Brand Chili Hot Dog Sauce
Wolf Brand Tamales in Chili Gravy
Wolf Brand Extra Spicy Chili without Beans

Van Camp's Brown Sugar Beans
Van Camp's Pork & Beans
Van Camp's Red Beans
Van Camp's Vegetarian Beans in Tomato Sauce
Van Camp's Beanee Weenee
Van Camp's Chilee Weenee
Van Camp's Western Style Beans
Van Camp's Baked Beans
Van Camp's Chili with Beans
Van Camp's Chili without Beans
Van Camp's Golden Hominy
Van Camp's Golden Hominy with Red and Green Peppers
Van Camp's White Hominy
Van Camp's Butter Beans
Van Camp's Dark Red Kidney Beans
Van Camp's Light Red Kidney Beans
Van Camp's New Orleans Style Red Kidney Beans
Van Camp's Mexican Style Chili Beans

Aunt Jemima Corn Muffin Mix
Aunt Jemima Blueberry Muffin Mix

Aunt Jemima Whole Wheat Pancake & Waffle Mix
Aunt Jemima Buckwheat Pancake & Waffle Mix
Aunt Jemima Corn Bread Easy Mix
Aunt Jemima Self-Rising Yellow Corn Meal Mix
Aunt Jemima Self-Rising White Corn Meal Mix - Bolted
Aunt Jemima Artificially Flavored Butter Lite Syrup
Aunt Jemima Coffee Cake Easy Mix
Aunt Jemima Lite Syrup
Aunt Jemima Pancake & Waffle Syrup
Aunt Jemima Pancake & Waffle Mix - Original
Aunt Jemima Enriched Self-Rising Flour
Aunt Jemima Enrich Bolted Self-Rising White Corn Meal
Aunt Jemima Enriched Degerminated Self-Rising White
     Corn Meal
Aunt Jemima Corn Meal White - Degerminated
Aunt Jemima Corn Meal Yellow - Degerminated

Gatorade Fruit Punch Flavor Mix
Gatorade Fruit Punch Flavor Drink
Gatorade Orange Flavor Drink
Gatorade Orange Flavor Mix
Gatorade Lemon-Lime Flavor Drink
Gatorade Lemon-Lime Flavor Mix
Gatorade Lemonade Flavor Drink

Quaker Scotch Barley - Regular
Quaker Scotch Barley - Quick Cooking
Quaker Instant Grits with Imitation Bacon Bits
Quaker Instant Grits with Imitation Ham Bits
Quaker Instant Grits
Quaker Hominy Grits - Regular, White
Quaker Hominy Grits - Quick, White
Quaker Hominy Grits - Quick, Yellow

Quaker Puffed Rice
Quaker Puffed Wheat
Cap'n Crunch Cereal
Cap'n Crunch Choco Crunch
Cap'n Crunch Peanut Butter Cereal
Quaker Unprocessed Bran
Quisp

Quaker Cinnamon Life
Quaker Raisin Life
Mr. T
Halfsies
Quaker Corn Bran (U.S)
Popeye Sweet Crunch
Popeye Sweet Puffs

Quaker Whole Wheat Natural Cereal
Quaker Creamy Wheat - Enriched Farina
Quaker Oat Bran
Quaker Old Fashioned Oats
Quaker Quick Oats
Mother's Instant Oatmeal (Non-Fortified)
Quaker Quick Oats with Apples, Raisins and Spice
Quaker Quick Oats with Raisin & Cinnamon
Quaker Apple, Raisin, and Walnut Instant Oatmeal
Quaker Apple, Honey and Walnut Instant Oatmeal
Quaker Instant Oatmeal with Real Apple and Artificial
          Apple Flavor and Cinnamon
Quaker Instant Oatmeal
Quaker Artificially Flavored Maple-Brown Sugar Instant
          Oatmeal
Quaker Raisin-Spice Instant Oatmeal
Quaker Cinnamon-Spice Instant Oatmeal
Quaker Instant Oatmeal with Real Honey & Graham
Quaker Raisin, Date and Walnut Instant Oatmeal
Masa Trigo
Quaker Enriched Masa Harina

Flako Corn Muffin Mix
Flako Pie Crust Mix

Plain Rice Cakes
Plain (Unsalted) Rice Cakes
Sesame Rice Cakes
Corn Rice Cakes
Multigrain Rice Cakes
Buckwheat (Unsalted) Rice Cakes
Barley & Oat Rice Cakes
Sesame (Unsalted) Rice Cakes

Rye Rice Cakes
Multigrain (Unsalted) Rice Cakes

For an update on lactose data, write:
The Quaker Oats Company
Consumer Response Department
Merchandise Mart Plaza
Chicago, IL 60654

RALSTON PURINA COMPANY
Rice Chex
Bran Chex
Corn Chex
Wheat Chex
Double Chex
Almond Delight
Honey Graham Chex
Sun Flakes
Chocolate-Chip Cookie-Crisp
Ralston 40% Bran Flakes
Ralston Corn Flakes
Ralston Raisin Bran
Ralston Sugar Frosted Flakes
Ralston High Fiber Hot cereal
Ralston Crispy Rice
Ralston Sugar Frosted Crispy Rice
Ralston Tasteeos
RyKrisp Crackers

For an update on lactose data, write:
Ralston Purina Company
Grocery Products Division
Office of Consumer Affairs
Checkerboard Square
St. Louis, MO 63164
(314) 982-2250

LOUIS RICH
Franks/Smoked Sausage
Turkey franks
Turkey smoked sausage

Sliced Meats
>Turkey bologna
>Turkey cotto salami
>Turkey ham
>Chopped and formed turkey ham
>Turkey luncheon loaf
>Oven roasted turkey breast
>Turkey pastrami
>Turkey salami
>Smoked turkey
>Smoked turkey breast

Natural Skin-on Boneless Breast of Turkey
>Barbecued breast of turkey
>Oven roasted breast of turkey
>Smoked breast of turkey

1-1/2 to 2 Pound Chunks
>Oven roasted turkey breast
>Smoked turkey breast
>Turkey ham
>Turkey pastrami
>Turkey salami
>Smoked turkey

For an update on lactose data, write:
>LOUIS RICH COMPANY
>Consumer Center
>P.O. Box 7188
>Madison, WI 53707
>(608) 241-6822

SANDOZ NUTRITION
>Resource®
>>Creamy Vanilla
>>Chocolate
>Citrotein®
>>Orange
>>Grape
>>Punch

For an update on lactose data, write:
> SANDOZ NUTRITION
> Clinical Nutrition Division
> 5320 West Twenty Third Street
> Minneapolis, MN 55416
> (800) 328-RUSH

SARA LEE

Sara Lee Bagels
> Poppyseed
> Egg
> Cinnamon & Raisin
> Onion
> Plain

Sara Lee Muffins
> Blueberry
> Oatmeal N Fruit
> Apple Cinnamon Spice
> Banana Nut Bran

For an update on lactose data, write:
> Consumer Services
> Kitchens of Sara Lee
> 500 Waukegan Road
> Deerfield, IL 60015

STOUFFER FOODS

REGULAR ENTREES
> Beef Chop Suey with Rice
> Beef Stew
> Beef Teriyaki with Rice and Vegetables
> Cashew Chicken with Rice
> Chicken Chow Mein
> Chili Con Carne
> Green Pepper Steak with Rice
> Macaroni and Beef with Tomatoes
> Roast Beef Hash
> Short Ribs of Beef with Vegetable Gravy
> Stuffed Green Peppers with Beef in Tomato
>> Sauce

LEAN CUISINE ENTREES
    Chicken a l'Orange with Almond Rice
    Chicken Cacciatore with Vermicelli
    Chicken Chow Mein with Rice
    Glazed Chicken with Vegetable Rice
    Linguini with Clam Sauce
    Meatball Stew
    Oriental Beef with Vegetables and Rice
    Oriental Scallops and Vegetables with Rice
    Stuffed Cabbage with Meat in Tomato Sauce

DINNER SUPREME
    Baked Chicken Breast
    Beef Teriyaki

SIDE DISHES
    Apple Pecan Rice
    Escalloped Apples
    Rice Medley
    Yams and Apples

SOUPS
    Split Pea with Ham

For an update on lactose data, write:
    STOUFFER FOODS CORPORATION
    Consumer Affairs Department
    5750 Harper Road
    Solon, OH 44139
    (216) 248-3600

SWIFT & COMPANY

Swift & Company does not maintain a listing of lactose-free foods. They responded: "Nutrition analysis of our products and up-dating nutrient information is an on-going process because of formulation changes and new product introductions. To provide consumers with current information which meets their specific needs, we prefer that they write directly to us. We will do our best to provide the information they need."

Write to:
Swift & Company
Consumer Communications
1919 Swift Drive
Oak Brook, IL 60521

WM. WRIGLEY JR. COMPANY

All Wrigley brands of chewing gums are lactose-free:
    Wrigley's Spearmint
    Doublemint
    Juicy Fruit
    Big Red
    Freedent
    Extra sugarfree gum
    Hubba Bubba bubble gum
    Hubba bubba sugarfree bubble gum

For an update on lactose data, write:
    Wm. Wrigley Jr. Company
    Wrigley Building
    410 North Michigan Avenue
    Chicago, IL 60611

NOTE: THE FOLLOWING LISTS OF PRODUCTS CONTAIN LACTOSE

BABY FOODS

BEECH-NUT NUTRITION CORPORATION

Beech-Nut produces 123 baby foods; only 22 contain lactose. Because of this extensive list, we deviate from the usual format. *Only those which contain lactose are listed.* All others are lactose-free as of this printing.

Beech-Nut Baby Foods which *contain* lactose:
>   Rice Cereal with Applesauce and Bananas
>   Beef Dinner Supreme
>   Vegetable Chicken Dinner
>   Macaroni, Tomato & Beef Dinner
>   Spaghetti, Tomato & Beef Dinner
>   Creamed Corn
>   Cottage Cheese with Pineapple
>   Mixed Fruit & Yogurt
>   Peaches & Yogurt
>   Banana Custard Pudding
>   Vanilla Custard Pudding
>   Dutch Apple Dessert
>   Banana Pineapple Dessert
>   Scalloped Potatoes
>   Table Time Beef Stew
>   Table Time Hearty Chicken with Stars Soup
>   Table Time Pasta Squares in Meat Sauce
>   Table Time Spaghetti Rings in Meat Sauce
>   Table Time Vegetable Stew with Chicken

All other Beech-Nut baby foods are lactose-free.

Medical and nutritional counseling are recommended for infants placed on a lactose-free diet. Infant feeding is beyond the scope of *The Milk Sugar Dilemma.*

For an update on lactose data, write:
>   Medical Services Department
>   The Beech-Nut Nutrition Corporation
>   Fort Washington, PA 19034

GERBER® BABY FOODS

The Gerber Products Company produces 159 baby foods, only 35 contain lactose. Because of this extensive list, we deviate from the usual format. *Only those which contain lactose are listed.* All others are lactose-free as of this printing.

Gerber Baby Foods which *contain* lactose:

Gerber Strained Foods
>   Creamed Corn
>   Creamed Spinach
>   Turkey with Vegetables
>   Cereal Egg Yolk with Bacon
>   Rice Cereal with Applesauce and Bananas
>   Chicken Noodle Dinner
>   Macaroni Cheese Dinner
>   Macaroni-Tomato Beef Dinner
>   Chocolate Custard Pudding
>   Dutch Apple Dessert
>   Hawaiian Delight
>   Orange Pudding
>   Vanilla Custard Pudding

Gerber Junior Foods
>   Creamed Corn
>   Creamed Green Beans
>   Turkey with Vegetables
>   Rice Cereal with Mixed Fruit
>   Spaghetti, Tomato Sauce Beef Dinner
>   Split Peas Ham Dinner
>   Vegetable Bacon Dinner
>   Chicken Sticks
>   Meat Sticks
>   Turkey Sticks
>   Home Style Noodles & Beef
>   Potatoes and Ham
>   Toddler Biter Biscuits
>   Spaghetti, Tomato Sauce & Beef
>   Vegetables & Chicken
>   Saucy Rice with Chicken

Cookies (Animal Shaped)
Zwieback Toast
Hawaiian Delight
Dutch Apple Dessert
Vanilla Custard Pudding
Arrowroot Cookies

All other Gerber baby foods are lactose-free.

Medical and nutritional counseling are recommended for infants placed on a lactose-free diet. Infant feeding is beyond the scope of *The Milk Sugar Dilemma.*

For an update on lactose data, write:
Gerber Products Company
Fremont, MI 49412

10
APPENDICES

I   RECOMMENDED DIETARY

Recommended Daily Dietary Allowances;[a] Revised 1980

Food and Nutrition Board, National Academy of Sciences—National Research Council

Designed for the maintenance of good nutrition of practically all healthy people in the U.S.A.

	Age (years)	Weight (kg)	Weight (lbs)	Height (cm)	Height (in)	Protein (g)	Fat-Soluble Vitamins			Water-Soluble Vitamins							Minerals					
							Vitamin A (µg RE) b	Vitamin D (µg) c	Vitamin E (mg α TE) d	Vitamin C (mg)	Thiamin (mg)	Riboflavin (mg)	Niacin (mg NE) e	Vitamin B6 (mg)	Folacin (µg) f	Vitamin B12 (µg)	Calcium (mg)	Phosphorus (mg)	Magnesium (mg)	Iron (mg)	Zinc (mg)	Iodine (µg)
Infants	0.0-0.5	6	13	60	24	kg × 2.2	420	10	3	35	0.3	0.4	6	0.3	30	0.5[g]	360	240	50	10	3	40
	0.5-1.0	9	20	71	28	kg × 2.0	400	10	4	35	0.5	0.6	8	0.6	45	1.5	540	360	70	15	5	50
Children	1-3	13	29	90	35	23	400	10	5	45	0.7	0.8	9	0.9	100	2.0	800	800	150	15	10	70
	4-6	20	44	112	44	30	500	10	6	45	0.9	1.0	11	1.3	200	2.5	800	800	200	10	10	90
	7-10	28	62	132	52	34	700	10	7	45	1.2	1.4	16	1.6	300	3.0	800	800	250	10	10	120
Males	11-14	45	99	157	62	45	1000	10	8	50	1.4	1.6	18	1.8	400	3.0	1200	1200	350	18	15	150
	15-18	66	145	176	69	56	1000	10	10	60	1.4	1.7	18	2.0	400	3.0	1200	1200	400	18	15	150
	19-22	70	154	177	70	56	1000	7.5	10	60	1.5	1.7	19	2.2	400	3.0	800	800	350	10	15	150
	23-50	70	154	178	70	56	1000	5	10	60	1.4	1.6	18	2.2	400	3.0	800	800	350	10	15	150
	51+	70	154	178	70	56	1000	5	10	60	1.2	1.4	16	2.2	400	3.0	800	800	350	10	15	150
Females	11-14	46	101	157	62	46	800	10	8	50	1.1	1.3	15	1.8	400	3.0	1200	1200	300	18	15	150
	15-18	55	120	163	64	46	800	10	8	60	1.1	1.3	14	2.0	400	3.0	1200	1200	300	18	15	150
	19-22	55	120	163	64	44	800	7.5	8	60	1.1	1.3	14	2.0	400	3.0	800	800	300	18	15	150
	23-50	55	120	163	64	44	800	5	8	60	1.0	1.2	13	2.0	400	3.0	800	800	300	18	15	150
	51+	55	120	163	64	44	800	5	8	60	1.0	1.2	13	2.0	400	3.0	800	800	300	10	15	150
Pregnant						+30	+200	+5	+2	+20	+0.4	+0.3	+2	+0.6	+400	+1.0	+400	+400	+150	h	+5	+25
Lactating						+20	+400	+5	+3	+40	+0.5	+0.5	+5	+0.5	+100	+1.0	+400	+400	+150	h	+10	+50

a The allowances are intended to provide for individual variations among most normal persons as they live in the United States under usual environmental stresses. Diets should be based on a variety of common foods in order to provide other nutrients for which human requirements have been less well defined. See p. 23 for heights, weights and recommended intake.

b Retinol equivalents. 1 Retinol equivalent = 1 µg retinol or 6 µg β carotene. See text for calculation

of vitamin A activity of diets as retinol equivalents.

c As cholecalciferol. 10 µg cholecalciferol = 400 I.U. vitamin D.

d α-tocopherol equivalents. 1 mg d-α-tocopherol = 1 α T.E. See text for variation in allowances and calculation of vitamin E activity of the diet as α-tocopherol equivalents.

e 1 N.E. (niacin equivalent) is equal to 1 mg of niacin or 60 mg of dietary tryptophan.

f The folacin allowances refer to dietary sources

as determined by *Lactobacillus casei* assay after treatment with enzymes ("conjugases") to make polyglutamyl forms of the vitamin available to the test organism.

g The RDA for vitamin B₁₂ in infants is based on an average concentration of the vitamin in human milk. The allowances after weaning are based on energy intake (as recommended by the American Academy of Pediatrics) and consideration of other factors such as intestinal absorption; see text.

h The increased requirement during pregnancy cannot be met by the iron content of habitual American diets nor by the existing iron stores of many women; therefore the use of 30-60 mg of supplemental iron is recommended. Iron needs during lactation are not substantially different from those of non-pregnant women, but continued supplementation of the mother for 2-3 months after parturition is advisable in order to replenish stores depleted by pregnancy.

ALLOWANCES (RDA)

Recommended Dietary Allowances, Revised 1980

Food and Nutrition Board, National Academy of Sciences—National Research Council, Washington, D.C.

Estimated Safe and Adequate Daily Dietary Intakes of Selected Vitamins and Minerals[a]

	Age (years)	Vitamins			Trace Elements[b]						Electrolytes		
		Vitamin K (µg)	Biotin (µg)	Pantothenic Acid (mg)	Copper (mg)	Manganese (mg)	Fluoride (mg)	Chromium (mg)	Selenium (mg)	Molybdenum (mg)	Sodium (mg)	Potassium (mg)	Chloride (mg)
Infants	0-0.5	12	35	2	0.5-0.7	0.5-0.7	0.1-0.5	0.01-0.04	0.01-0.04	0.03-0.06	115-350	350-925	275-700
	0.5-1	10-20	50	3	0.7-1.0	0.7-1.0	0.2-1.0	0.02-0.06	0.02-0.06	0.04-0.08	250-750	425-1275	400-1200
Children	1-3	15-30	65	3	1.0-1.5	1.0-1.5	0.5-1.5	0.02-0.08	0.02-0.08	0.05-0.1	325-975	550-1650	500-1500
and	4-6	20-40	85	3-4	1.5-2.0	1.5-2.0	1.0-2.5	0.03-0.12	0.03-0.12	0.06-0.15	450-1350	775-2325	700-2100
Adolescents	7-10	30-60	120	4-5	2.0-2.5	2.0-3.0	1.5-2.5	0.05-0.2	0.05-0.2	0.1-0.3	600-1800	1000-3000	925-2775
	11+	50-100	100-200	4-7	2.0-3.0	2.5-5.0	1.5-2.5	0.05-0.2	0.05-0.2	0.15-0.5	900-2700	1525-4575	1400-4200
Adults		70-140	100-200	4-7	2.0-3.0	2.5-5.0	1.5-4.0	0.05-0.2	0.05-0.2	0.15-0.5	1100-3300	1875-5625	1700-5100

a Because there is less information on which to base allowances, these figures are not given in the main table of the RDA and are provided here in the form of ranges of recommended intakes.

b Since the toxic levels for many trace elements may be only several times usual intakes, the upper levels for the trace elements given in this table should not be habitually exceeded.

Mean Heights and Weights and Recommended Energy Intake[a] Recommended Dietary Allowances, Revised 1980

Category	Age (years)	Weight (kg)	Weight (lb)	Height (cm)	Height (in)	Energy Needs (with range) [kcal]	(MJ)
Infants	0.0-0.5	6	13	60	24	kg × 115 (95-145)	kg × .48
	0.5-1.0	9	20	71	28	kg × 105 (80-135)	kg × .44
Children	1-3	13	29	90	35	1300 (900-1800)	5.5
	4-6	20	44	112	44	1700 (1300-2300)	7.1
	7-10	28	62	132	52	2400 (1650-3300)	10.1
Males	11-14	45	99	157	62	2700 (2000-3700)	11.3
	15-18	66	145	176	69	2800 (2100-3900)	11.8
	19-22	70	154	177	70	2900 (2500-3300)	12.2
	23-50	70	154	178	70	2700 (2300-3100)	11.3
	51-75	70	154	178	70	2400 (2000-2800)	10.1
	76+	70	154	178	70	2050 (1650-2450)	8.6
Females	11-14	46	101	157	62	2200 (1500-3000)	9.2
	15-18	55	120	163	64	2100 (1200-3000)	8.8
	19-22	55	120	163	64	2100 (1700-2500)	8.8
	23-50	55	120	163	64	2000 (1600-2400)	8.4
	51-75	55	120	163	64	1800 (1400-2200)	7.6
	76+	55	120	163	64	1600 (1200-2000)	6.7
Pregnancy						+300	
Lactation						+500	

a The data in this table have been assembled from the observed median heights and weights of children shown in Table 1, together with desirable weights for adults given in Table 2 for the mean heights of men (70 inches) and women (64 inches) between the ages of 18 and 34 years as surveyed in the U.S. population (HEW/NCHS data).

The energy allowances for the young adults are for men and women doing light work. The allowances for the two older groups represent mean energy needs over these age spans, allowing for a 2% decrease in basal (resting) metabolic rate per decade and a reduction in activity of 200 kcal/day for men and women between 51 and 75 years, 500 kcal for men over 75 years and 400 kcal for women over 75 (see text). The customary range of daily energy output is shown for adults in parentheses, and is based on a variation in energy needs of ± 400 kcal at any one age (see text and Garrow, 1978), emphasizing the wide range of energy intakes appropriate for any group of people.

Energy allowances for children through age 18 are based on median energy intakes of children of these ages followed in longitudinal growth studies. The values in parentheses are the 10th and 90th percentiles of energy intake, to indicate the range of energy consumption among children of these ages (see text).

II LACTOSE-RESTRICTED DIET

ACCEPTABLE CHOICES

AVOID OR USE SPARINGLY

Beverages

Vitamite®, Lactaid®, coffee, Postum®, tea, Coffee Rich®, carbonated beverages, fruit drinks if lactose-free, instant iced tea if 100% tea; soybean milks such as Soyagen®, Soyamel®, Isomil®, Nursoy®, NeoMullsoy®, and ProSobee®; Sustacal®, Ensure®. Alcoholic beverages (except wines with added sugar), cocoa powder or Nestle's Quik, if mixed with water or milk substitute. Buttermilk, if tolerated.

Whole milk, low fat milk, skim milk, powdered milk, sweetened condensed milk, chocolate milk, instant chocolate, instant iced tea mixes; Ovaltine®, chocolate drink mixes, cream, half and half; fruit drinks if they contain lactose; wine with sugar added, some cordials and liqueurs.

Breads, Rolls & Cereals

Water-base bread or rolls (most Italian, French, Vienna, or Jewish rye bread), Hillbilly® bread, most Schafer's® breads; Ry-Krisp®, some crackers such as Ritz® or Zesta®; graham crackers, rusk, and other crackers without milk products; almost any Jewish bakery product. Any kind of cereal, cooked or dry, if no lactose is added; infant cereals without lactose or milk solids added.

Bread and rolls to which milk or lactose is added; biscuits, muffins, pancakes, sweet rolls, doughnuts, waffles, hamburger and hot dog buns unless made without milk. Instant cereals, cereals such as Special K® and Cocoa Krispies® to which milk products have been added.

Desserts and Fruits

Any made without milk or milk products such as angel food cake, gelatin desserts, most fruit pies, fruit ices, homemade cakes and cookies made from acceptable ingredients. Packaged mixes for cakes, puddings, etc. without lactose, whey, or milk solids. Any fresh fruit, or canned, frozen, or dried. Yogurt, if tolerated.

Commercial desserts and others prepared with milk and milk products; pudding, sherbet, and ice cream; most chocolate desserts; most soufflés and mousses, strained infant desserts.

ACCEPTABLE CHOICES

AVOID OR USE SPARINGLY

Fats, Oils, & Nuts

Bacon, butter, milk-free margarine such as Shedd's Spread®, Diet Imperial®, Willow Run®; diet imitation margarine, salad dressings without milk solids; vegetable oils and shortenings, olives, mayonnaise; non-dairy cream, such as Coffeemate® Coffee Rich®, and whipped toppings without milk products added. Any kind of nuts.

Most dairy and non-dairy coffee creamers, sour cream, cream cheese, margarine containing milk solids; chip dips, sauces and salad dressings containing milk or milk products.

Meats and Substitutes

Any plain meat, fish, poultry, or eggs except those listed to be avoided; Kosher prepared meat products; peanut butter, Ball Park® frankfurters and other sausage products without milk solids; soybean meat substitutes; dried peas, beans, and lentils prepared without milk or milk products; hard, ripened cheeses such as Blue, Brick, Brie, Cheddar, Colby, Edam, Gouda, Monterey, Parmesan and Swiss. Cottage cheese, ricotta, or mozzarella, if tolerated.

Breaded or creamed eggs, fish, meat, or poultry; luncheon meats, sausage, liver sausage and frankfurters containing milk solids; unripened cheese such as cream cheese.

Potatoes and Starches

Macaroni, noodles, rice, spaghetti, white and sweet potatoes, except as listed to avoid.

Creamed and escalloped potatoes, au gratin potatoes, and instant potatoes and other commercial products with milk added; macaroni-cheese mixes.

Seasonings

Any, except those listed to be avoided; monosodium glutamate, if 100% pure.

Condiments with lactose added; some spice blends.

Soups

Bouillon, broth and meat stock soups; "cream soups," bisques and chowders made with water or soy milk.

Cream soups, canned and dehydrated soup mixes if lactose is added.

ACCEPTABLE CHOICES	AVOID OR USE SPARINGLY
Sweets and Candies	
Brown, granulated, and powdered sugar; corn syrup, honey, jams, jellies, hard candies, and any candy made without milk, lactose, or margarine.	Chocolate and cream candies, toffee, peppermints, butterscotch, caramels; sugar substitutes with lactose added.
Vegetables	
Fresh, frozen and canned without milk or milk products.	Creamed or breaded vegetables, or vegetables with margarine added.
Miscellaneous	
Popcorn, pretzels, mustard, catsup and pickles; gravies and sauces made without milk or milk products; flavorings and extracts.	Chewing gum, Korn Kurls®. and any product containing milk, lactose, whey, dry milk solids, nonfat dry milk; cream sauces, milk gravy; ascorbic acid tablets or citric acid mixture containing lactose.

ABOUT THE LACTOSE-RESTRICTED DIET

Lactose is a unique sugar which occurs *naturally* only in milk. It dissolves easily and is less sweet than other sugars. As a consequence, it is often used in commercial food products. Many tablets and pills contain lactose, but usually in trace amounts.

The LACTOSE-RESTRICTED DIET is composed of two food lists: ACCEPTABLE CHOICES and AVOID OR USE SPARINGLY. For a trial period of at least four to five days, it is recommended that you make your food selections only from ACCEPTABLE CHOICES to ensure that your diet will be lactose-free. Once symptoms are controlled, individual experimentation is encouraged to determine your own individual tolerance to lactose. Your choices may well include some foods on the AVOID OR USE SPARINGLY list. For some individuals, tolerance to lactose may diminish over time. A trial return to the lactose-free diet, with reintroduction of foods, may be necessary.

In certain medical situations, it is advisable to avoid coffee, tea, colas, caffeine, chocolate, alcohol, nuts, and popcorn. Check with your physician regarding his recommendations for your case.

Lactaid® is available in health food stores and pharmacies. It is the enzyme (lactase) which splits the milk sugar (lactose) into two sugars which are readily absorbed. Enzyme-treated milk is 70-90%

lactose-free, depending on the number of drops added, and has a slightly sweeter taste than untreated milk.

Vitamite® is a non-diary drink that tastes rather like milk, contains 1/2 the calcium, and may be used in place of milk as a beverage or in cooking. It can be purchased in the dairy section of grocery stores.

Fermented or cultured milk products such as cottage cheese, ricotta cheese, yogurt, and buttermilk are often tolerated by lactose-intolerant individuals. On the initial trial diet, these should be avoided. After symptoms are controlled, these foods may be tried.

Natural aging of cheese minimizes its lactose content. (In the making of cheese, most of the lactose is removed in the whey as it is separated out. In the final ripening process, the small amount of lactose still included is transformed into an easily digested by-product. Hence, most of the aged cheese products are well tolerated. Unlikely to be tolerated are American and processed cheese, cheese spreads, imitation cheese and cheese foods. These are not aged; also, extra milk solids have been added.

All labels hould be read carefully for the addition of lactose, whey, milk, dry milk solids, and nonfat dry milk. Lactose-free food information is also available in lists from various food companies. Incidentally, lactalbumin, lactate, and certain calcium compounds are often mention on labels. These do not contain lactose.

If you need to avoid milk for any length of time, taking vitamins containing calcium and Vitamin D is advised. Additional quantities are necessary during pregnancy and nursing. These non-prescription tablets can be purchased at any pharmacy.

The LACTOSE-RESTRICTED DIET is taken from THE MILK SUGAR DILEMMA: LIVING WITH LACTOSE INTOL-ERANCE, by Richard A. Martens, M.D, and Sherlyn Martens, M.S., R.D. The book is published by MEDI-ED PRESS, Post Office Box 957, East Lansing, Michigan 48826-0957. Price: $13.95 + $1.50 shipping. 260 pages, indexed.

Table of Contents of THE MILK SUGAR DILEMMA: Lactose Intolerance, Digestion, Nutritional Guidelines, The Lactose-Restricted Diet, Setting Your Lactose Level, Shopping for Foods, Dining Away From Home, Recipes, Lactose-free Food Products.

Note: The LACTOSE-RESTRICTED DIET is not copyrighted. It may be duplicated and distributed as desired.

III

TABLE OF SELECTED NUTRIENT
CONTENT OF VARIOUS FOODS

The following table contains nutrient information for various foods pertinent to the planning of a lactose-restricted diet. The selected nutrients include those which are likely to be deficient if milk is simply omitted from the diet (see SECTION 3). The nutrients in milk are shown in bold print in the Milk Group. In order to replace milk, the substitute should approach the nutritive value of milk. If this is not possible, a combination of foods can be selected to provide these nutrients. The selected nutrients include calories, protein, Vitamin A, Vitamin D, riboflavin, and calcium. Vitamin C is included in the Fruit and Vegetable Group to assist in menu planning. For additional nutrient information, the reader is referred to *Food Values of Portions Commonly Used*, by Pennington and Church.

MILK AND MILK SUBSTITUTE GROUP

FOOD	PORTION SIZE	CALORIES	PROTEIN Grams	VIT.A IU	VIT.D IU	RIBO Mg	CALCIUM Mg
Buttermilk	1 cup	99	8	81	-	0.38	285
Cheddar Cheese	1 oz.	114	7	300	-	tr	204
Colby Cheese	1 oz.	112	7	293	-	0.11	194
Cottage Cheese	4 oz.	117	14	184	2	0.18	68
Ensure®	1 cup	245	9	625	50	0.43	130
Ensure Plus®	1 cup	355	13	890	70	0.65	150
Frogurt®	1/2 cup	100	3	tr	-	0.08	56
Isocal®	1 cup	240	8	625	50	0.54	150
Isomil®	1 cup	240	7	500	100	0.15	230
Lactaid®	1 cup	80-170	8	307	100	0.39	291
Milk,sk or wh	1 cup	80-170	8	307	100	0.39	291
Ricotta Cheese	1/2 cup	171	15	608	-	0.24	257
Soyagen®	1 cup	130	6	-	50	0.17	150
Soyamel®	1 cup	130	5.6	105	50	0.48	240
Sustacal®	1 cup	240	15	1110	89	0.40	240
Swiss Cheese	1 oz	107	8	240	-	0.10	272
Vitamite®	1 cup	120	3	500	100	-	160
Yogurt, fruited	1 cup	225	10	104	-	0.40	345
Yogurt,plain	1 cup	144	12	150	-	0.49	415

PROTEIN GROUP

FOOD	PORTION SIZE	CALORIES	PROTEIN grams	VIT.A IU	VIT.D IU	RIBO mg	CALCIUM mg
Beef	3.5 oz	261	26	30	-	0.22	12
Chicken	3.5 oz	193	29	91	-	0.12	14
Egg	1 .large.	79	7	260	27	0.14	28
Ham	3.5 oz	306	32	0	0	0.27	6
Lamb	3.5 oz	242	20.6	0	0	0.22	6
Lentils cooked	2/3 cup	106	8	20		0.06	25
Lima Beans, froz,	1/2 .cup	128	7	219	-	0.07	33
Liver, fried	3.5 oz	229	26	53,400	14	4.19	11
Oysters, canned	3.5 oz	76	9	440	-	0.29	152
Peanut Butter	2 T.	186	9	0	0	0.04	13
Pork	3.5 oz	306	33	0	0	0.27	6
Salmon, sockeye	3.5 oz	171	20.3	230	-	0.06	260*
Sardines in oil	8 med	311	21	180	-	0.16	354*
Shrimp	3.5 oz	116	25	60	-	0.03	115
Smelt, canned	5 med	200	18	-	-	0.12	358*
Tofu, soy curd	3.5 oz	72	8	0	-	0.03	128
Turkey	3.5 oz	155	21	-	-	0.16	5
Veal	3.5 oz	234	26	0	0	0.25	11
Nuts & Seeds							
Almonds	12-15	90	3	0	0	0.10	38
Filberts	10-12	97	1.6	16	0	0.08	38
Peanuts, roasted	1 oz.	158	8	tr	-	0.04	10
Sesame seeds	1 tbsp.	47	2	5	-	0.10	10
Sunflower seeds	1 tbsp.	157	7	12	-	0.06	34

*Calcium values include soft edible bones.
Note: 3.5 oz. is one medium serving.

GRAIN GROUP

FOOD	PORTION SIZE	CALORIES	PROTEIN Grams	VIT.A IU	VIT.D IU	RIBO Mg	CALCIUM Mg
BREAD							
Bagel	1	163	6	0	-	0.16	23
English Muffin	1 whole	135	4.5	0	-	0.18	92
French Bread	1 slice	70	2.4	tr	-	0.09	28
Italian Bread	1 slice	55	1.8	0	-	0.05	3
Rolls, Buns	1 large	137	4.3	tr	-	0.18	8
Rye, pumpernick	1 slice	82	3	0	-	0.17	23
Tortilla	1	67	2.1	-	-	0.14	42
Vienna Bread	1 slice	70	2.4	tr	-	0.09	28
Wheat, cracked	1 slice	66	2.3	tr	-	0.18	8
White Bread	1 slice	64	2	tr	-	0.07	30
CEREAL							
Cereal, ready to eat, enriched	1 cup	110	2	1250	-	0.40	1
Cereal, cooked	1 cup	108	5	29	-	0.04	15
Pasta, cooked	1 cup	216	7.3	0	-	0.15	16
Rice or Barley	4/5 cup	164	3	0	-	0.10	15
Wheat Germ	1/4 cup	108	8.3	-	-	0.23	13
CRACKERS							
Graham Crackers	2 squares	60	2	tr	-	0.04	5
Pretzels	1-oz bag	111	2.6	0	-	0.07	7
Saltines	2 crax	26	.6	0	-	0.03	4
FLOURS							
Flour, wheat	1 cup	400	11.6	0	-	0.43	20
Cornstarch	1 Tbsp	35	tr	-	-	-	-
Cornmeal	1 cup	120	2.6	144	-	0.10	2

FRUIT AND VEGETABLE GROUP

FOOD	PORTION SIZE	CALORIES	PROTEIN Grams	VIT.A IU	VIT.D IU	RIBO Mg	CALCIUM Mg	VIT C Mg
FRUIT								
Apple, raw	1 med	81	1.3	74	-	0.02	10	8
Apple juice	8 oz	111	.3	2	-	0.04	14	1
Applesauce	1/2 cup	97	.2	14	-	0.04	5	2
Apricots, raw	3 med	51	1	2770	-	0.04	15	11
Banana	1 med	105	1.2	92	-	0.11	7	10
Blueberries, raw	1 cup	82	1	145	-	0.07	9	19
Cantaloupe	1 cup	57	.7	3400	-	0.03	14	68
Cherries, canned	1/2 cup	68	1.1	156	-	0.03	17	3
Cranberries	1 cup	46	.4	44	-	0.02	7	13
Dates	10	228	1.6	42	-	0.08	27	0
Figs, canned	3	75	.3	31	-	0.03	18	1
Grapefruit, pink	1/2	37	.7	318	-	0.03	13	47
Grapefruit juice	1 cup	93	1.3	18	-	0.05	18	72
Grapes, raw	1 cup	58	.6	92	-	0.05	13	4
Grape juice	1 cup	155	1.4	20	-	0.09	22	tr
Honeydew	1/4	33	.8	40	-	0.03	14	23
Kiwi Fruit	1 med	46	.8	133	-	0.04	20	75
Lemon	1 med	17	.6	17	-	0.01	15	31
Lime	1 med	20	.5	7	-	0.01	22	20
Mango	1 med	135	1.1	8060	-	0.12	21	57
Nectarine	1 med	67	1.3	1001	-	0.06	6	7
Orange	1 med	59	1.3	278	-	0.05	48	59
Orange Juice	1 cup	112	1.7	194	-	0.05	22	97
Papaya	1 med	117	1.9	6122	-	0.10	72	188
Peach	1 med	37	.6	465	-	0.04	5	6
Pear	1 med	98	.7	33	-	0.07	19	7
Pineapple, raw	1 cup	77	.6	35	-	0.06	11	24
Pineapple juice	1 cup	129	1	25	-	0.05	28	30
Plums, raw	1 med	36	.5	213	-	0.06	2	6
Prunes, dried	10	201	2.2	1669	-	0.14	43	3
Prune juice	1 cup	181	1.6	9	-	0.18	30	11
Raisins	2/3 cup	300	3	8	-	0.09	49	3
Strawberries	1 cup	45	.9	42	-	0.10	21	85
Tangarine	1 med	37	.5	773	-	0.02	12	77
Watermelon	1 cup	50	1	585	-	0.03	13	15

FRUIT AND VEGETABLE GROUP, continued

FOOD	PORTION SIZE	CALORIES	PROTEIN Grams	VIT.A IU	VIT.D IU	RIBO Mg	CALCIUM Mg	VIT C Mg
VEGETABLES								
Asparagus	2/3 cup	20	2.2	900	-	0.18	21	26
Avocado	1 med	306	3.6	1059	-	0.21	19	24
Bean sprouts	1 cup	35	6	80	-	0.20	48	16
Beans, baked,cnd	8 oz	255	11	345	-	0.05	131	3
Beets, cooked	1/2 cup	27	.9	17	-	0.03	12	5
Broccoli	1 lg stalk	26	3	2500	-	0.20	88	90
Brussels sprouts	1 cup	35	6	80	-	0.20	48	138
Cabbage,shredded	1 cup	24	1.3	130	-	0.05	49	47
Carrots	2/3 cup	31	1	10,500	-	0.05	33	6
Cauliflower, ckd	7/8 cup	22	2.3	60	-	0.08	21	55
Celery, raw	1 stalk	8	.4	120	-	0.02	20	5
Corn	1/2 cup	88	3	238	-	0.06	5	6
Cucumbers	1/2 med	8	.5	125	-	0.02	13	6
Eggplant, cooked	1/2 cup	19	1	10	-	0.04	11	3
Green beans,ckd	2/3 cup	29	1.6	520	-	0.08	43	3
Green pepper, raw	1 large	22	1.2	420	-	0.08	9	128
Lima beans, frzn	1/2 cup	128	.7	219	-	0.07	33	18
Mushrooms, raw	10 sm	28	3	tr	-	0.46	6	3
Okra, cooked	8-9 pods	29	2	490	-	0.18	92	20
Onions, cooked	1/2 cup	29	1.2	40	-	0.03	24	7
Peas, green ckd	2/3 cup	71	5.4	540	-	0.11	23	20
Potatoes, bkd	1 large	139	3.9	tr	-	0.06	14	30
Pumpkin	2/5 cup	33	.9	33,990	-	0.06	18	5
Rhubarb, raw	1 cup	29	.8	147	-	0.04	266	7
Rutabaga, raw	1/2 cup	35	.9	550	-	0.06	59	26
Snow peas	6 oz	90	5.8	-	-	-	-	-
Spinach, cooked	1/2 cup	21	2.7	7300	-	0.13	83	25
Summer squash	1/2 cup	14	.9	390	-	0.08	25	10
Sweet potato	1 small	172	3	11,940	-	0.09	48	18
Tomatoes, raw	1 med	33	1.6	1350	-	0.06	20	34
Turnip greens,ckd	2/3 cup	20	2	6300	-	0.24	184	69
Wax beans	1/2 cup	22	1.4	230	-	0.09	50	13
Winter squash	1/2 cup	63	2	4200	-	0.13	28	20
Zucchini, frozen	1/2 cup	16	1.1	459	-	0.04	17	4

EXTRA CHOICES

FOOD	PORTION SIZE	CALORIES	PROTEIN grams	VIT.A IU	VIT.D IU	RIBO mg	CALCIUM mg
Angelfood cake	1/12 Cake	126	3.2	0	-	0.11	44
Bacon, fried	1 slice	35	1.6	0	-	0.02	tr
Bouillon	1 cup	19	1.3	4	-	0.02	5
Broth	1 cup	19	1.3	4	-	0.02	5
Butter	1 tbsp.	108	0.1	459	-	0.01	3
Carbonated bev	12 oz.	144	0	-	-	-	0
Catsup	1 tbsp.	16	0.3	210	-	0.01	3
Coffee	6 oz.	3	tr	0	-	0.02	13
Coffeemate®	1 tbsp	11	0.1	4	-	tr	tr
Coffee Rich®	1/2 oz.	20	0.2	13	-	0.00	1
Fish liver oils	1/8 oz.	-	-	-	500	-	-
French dressing	1 tbsp.	67	0.1	-	-	-	2
Fruit ice	1 cup	247	0.8	tr	-	tr	tr
Fruit pie, apple	1/8 pie	282	2.4	22	-	0.09	11
Gelatin, flavored	1/2 cup	81	1.6	0	-	0.00	tr
Gum	1 stick	10	0	0	-	0.00	3
Hard candy	6 pieces	66	0	0	0	0	3
Herbs (other nutrients neglible)							
Chili powder	1 tsp.			908			
Paprika	1 tsp.			1273			
Parsley	1 tbsp.			303			
Italian dressing	1 tbsp.	69	0.1	-	-	-	1
Jam, jelly	1 tbsp.	55	0.01	2	-	tr	2
Margarine	1 tbsp.	100	0.1	495	-	0.00	3
Mayonnaise	1 tbsp.	99	0.2	-	-	-	2
Pickles, dill	1 large	11	0.7	100	-	0.02	26
Tea	8 oz.	0	-	-	-	0.02	-
Vegetable oil	1 tbsp.	120	0	-	-	0	1
Vinegar	1 tbsp.	2	0	0	-	0	1

(-) indicates no data available
(tr) indicates trace amounts

Source: *Bowes and Church's Food Values of Portions Commonly Used,* Pennington and Church, 14th edition, J. B. Lippincott Company, Philadelphia, 1985

IV LACTOSE CONTENT OF VARIOUS FOODS

FOOD	LACTOSE (GRAMS)
Milk, in 1 cup servings	
Whole milk*	11
Low fat milk*	9-13
Buttermilk*	9-11
Chocolate milk*	10-12
Fortified skim milk*	12-14
Eggnog	14
Human milk	13.8
Goat milk	9.4
Sweetened condensed milk*	35
Evaporated milk, undiluted	20
Low sodium milk	9
Nonfat dry milk powder*	48
Yogurt*	11-15
Cream	
Half and half, 1/2 cup	5
Heavy whipping, 1/2 cup	3.1
Sour cream, 1/2 cup	3.2
Cream cheese, 1 ounce	.6
Cheese	
Cheese, aged, 1 oz.*	.1-.8
American Cheese Food, 1 oz.	2.4
Cheddar, 1 oz.	.6
Swiss, 1 oz.	.5
Cottage Cheese, creamed,1/2 c	2.4

FOOD	LACTOSE (GRAMS)
Cottage cheese, lowfat, 1/2 c	3.6
Cottage cheese, dry curd, 1/2 c	.8

Desserts

Ice milk, 1/2 cup	6-7.5
Ice cream, 1/2 cup	5-7
Milk chocolate, 3 oz.	8.1
Sherbet, 1/2 cup	2
Ices, 1/2 cup	0
Ice cream sandwich	2.4
Orange Creame Bar	3.1
Fudge Bar	4.9

Spreads

Butter, 1 teaspoon	trace (0.06)
Margarine with milk solids, 1 tsp.	.9

All other natural foods without added lactose, whey, or milk	0

The data were obtained from three sources: Lactose Content of Sealtest Food Products, and Michigan State University Nutrient Data Bank, 1984. Those indicated by an asterisk (*) are from *American Journal of Clinical Nutrition* 31:592, 1978. (Although the fermented dairy products contain lactose, they are tolerated by many lactose-intolerant individuals. See explanation in SECTION 3.)

V REFERENCES

Basic Nutrition Facts, edited and published by Michigan Department of Public Health, Lansing, Michigan, 1980.

Bowes & Church's Food Values of Portions Commonly Used, Pennington and Church, 14th edition, J. B. Lippincott Company, 1985.

Food Selection for Vegetarians, Fanelli, M.T. and Kuczmarski, R. J., *Dietetic Currents*, Ross Laboratories, Columbus, Ohio, January, 1983.

Lactase Deficiency, Necomer, Albert D., M. D., *Contemporary Nutrition*, Volume 4:4, Minneapolis, Minnesota, April, 1979.

Lactose Digestion, Clinical and Nutritional Implications, David M. Paige, M. D., M.P.H., and Theodore M. Bayless, M. D., editors. The Johns Hopkins University Press, Baltimore and London, 1981.

Lactose Intolerance and Yogurt, Part 1--Understanding the Problem, M.D. Levitt and D.A. Savaiano, *Practical Gastroenterology*, Volume 9, No. 1, January/February, 1985.

Lactose Intolerance and Yogurt, Part 2--Diagnosis and Treatment, M.D. Levitt and D.A. Savaiano, *Practical Gastroenterology,* Volume 9, No. 2, March/April, 1985.

Treatment of Lactose Intolerance - *The Medical Newsletter*, The Medical Letter, Inc., New Rochelle, N.Y.   p. 67-68, 1980.

VI RECIPE SOURCES

Several of the recipes were taken from or adapted from booklets prepared by milk substitute manufacturers. These can be obtained by writing directly to the company.

Cooking with Isomil®
Good Eating for the Person Sensitive to Cows' Milk or Other Foods (directed to milk allergy; therefore, recipes are lactose-free).
Ross Laboratories
625 Cleveland Avenue
Columbus, OH 43216

Consumer Relations Department
Hershey Foods Corporation
P.O. Box 815
Hershey, PA 17033-0815
Hershey's recipes courtesy of Hershey's Kitchens and reprinted with permission of Hershey Foods Corporation. Hershey's is a registered trademark of Hershey Foods Corporation.

LactAid® Patient Information Packet
LactAid, Inc.
P.O.Box 111
Pleasantville, NJ 08232-0111

Lacteeze Recipes
Kingsmill Diet Foods
1399 Kennedy Road
Scarborough, Ontario M1P 2L6

Seventeen Scrumptious Recipes Using Sustacal® and
Recipes Using Isocal®
(Some of these recipes use ice cream and other lactose-containing ingredients. Use only those which are lactose-free.)
Mead Johnson and Company
Evansville, IN 47721

Soyamel® Facts and Recipes
Worthington Foods
Worthington, OH 43085

VII GLOSSARY OF TERMS

absorption the movement of nutrients out of the digestive tract and into blood or lymph vessels of the villi.

amino acids the building blocks of protein.

bile a substance produced by the liver to help dissolve fats so they can be digested.

bowel resection surgery which removes part of the intestinal tract or bowel.

calcium a silver-white mineral, one form of which is found in milk, milk products, dark green leafy vegetables, needed by mammals to form healthy bones and teeth; also needed for blood clotting mechanisms and healthy nerve function.

calorie abbreviated Cal, also called kilocalorie, used to express the heat output of an organism and the fuel or energy value of food.

celiac sprue an inherited disease of the small intestine, in which an inability to tolerate gluten (the protein of wheat, oats, rye, and barley), leads to diarrhea, weight loss, cramping and bloating. It is diagnosed by a biopsy of the small intestine and is treated with a gluten-free diet. Often, a lactose-free diet is necessary as well.

colon the large intestine.

curd the solid portion of milk after the fluid has been removed. It is composed primarily of protein and certain minerals.

diarrhea the too frequent occurrence of too loose stools.

digestion the chemical breakdown of food into small molecules.

duodenum the first part of the small intestine immediately after the stomach.

enzyme a protein that serves as a catalyst in speeding chemical reactions in living things.

esophagus   a muscular tube extending from the mouth to the stomach.

fermentation   a change in a food brought about by yeast, mold, or certain bacteria.

gall bladder   a small sac on the underside of the right lobe of the liver that stores bile.

gastroenterology   the study of the structure and diseases of digestive organs.

gastrointestinal   of, pertaining to, or affecting the stomach and intestines.

genetics   the science of inheritance.

ileum   a part of the small intestine just prior to entry into the large intestine.

inflammatory bowel disease   a group of gastrointestinal diseases, such as Crohn's disease and ulcerative colitis, which are frequently characterized by diarrhea, cramping, and bleeding, due to damage to the intestinal lining.

kilocalorie   abbreviated kcal, also called calorie, used to express the heat output of an organism and the fuel or energy value of food.

kosher   Judaism: fit or allowed to be eaten or used, according to the dietary or ceremonial laws.

lactase   the enzyme which splits lactose (milk sugar) into 2 sugars: glucose and galactose; lactase is located in cells of the small intestine.

lactose   1. the 2-unit sugar (disaccharide) present in mammallian milk, which upon splitting yields glucose and galactose. 2. a white crystalline sweet, water-soluble commercial form of this compound, obtained from whey, used in infant feedings, confections and other foods, in bacteriological media, and in pharmacy as filler and as a binding agent. Also called milk sugar.

lactose-free not containing lactose or milk sugar.

lactose intolerance the inability to digest milk sugar or lactose, characterized by gaseousness, bloating, cramping and diarrhea.

large intestine the organ connected directly to the ileum of the small intestine. Its function is to reabsorb water and certain minerals from the waste products of digestion.

liver a large, soft, reddish-brown organ in the upper right side of the abdominal cavity where bile is produced and where various metabolic processes take place.

malabsorption improper or incomplete absorption of digested foods.

maldigestion improper or incomplete digestion of foods.

metabolism the sum of all the chemical reactions involved in life's activities.

milk solids milk with only the water removed. Includes nonfat dry milk, dry milk powder, and nonfat dry milk powder.

minerals inorganic substances that are essential for good health.

nutrients vitamins, minerals, protein, fat, carbohydrate, and water, essential to good health.

nutrition the intake and use of food by living things for energy, growth, or repair.

nutritious diet a meal plan that contains all the ingredients necessary for maintaining good health.

pancreas the organ that lies behind the stomach and duodemum. It produces enzymes that help to digest food. It also produces hormones that help regulate the amount of sugar in the blood.

pareve Judaism: permissible for use with both meat and dairy meals; neutral.

peristalsis   waves of muscle contractions that serve to squeeze food through the digestive tract.

pylorus the opening between the stomach and the duodenum.

protein any of a group of nitrogen-containing organic compounds which yield amino acids and that are required for all life processes in animals.

riboflavin Vitamin B_2, a chemical substance found in milk, meat, eggs, leafy vegetables, enriched grain products; essential for growth.

saliva fluid secreted into the mouth by the salivary glands to moisten and soften food so that it is easier to swallow. Also contains a starch-digesting enzyme to begin the digestive process.

saturated fat   a fat in which each carbon atom in the fatty acid chain (except the end carbon atoms) is bonded to two hydrogen atoms; usually found in animal fats, a high intake of which is a factor in heart disease and atherosclerosis.

small intestine   a narrow tube about 2.5 centimeters in diameter and 3-5 meters long, into which food passes from the stomach. Many aspects of digestion of fat, protein, and carbohydrate occur here.

stomach a J-shaped elastic bag in the upper left portion of the abdominal cavity between the esophagus and the duodenum.

unsaturated fat   a fat which is not saturated with hydrogen; usually found in vegetable oils. A diet consisting of moderate amounts of unsaturated fats in place of saturated fats may be preventive in heart disease.

villi   **(singular, villus)**   structures on the intestinal lining which extend into the hollow of the intestine and increase the surface area for absorption of digested food.

Vitamin A   a chemical substance obtained from green and yellow vegetables, egg yolk, etc., essential to growth, the portection of skin, and prevention of night blindness.

Vitamin B$_2$ riboflavin, a chemical substance found in milk, meat, eggs, leafy vegetables, enriched grain products; essential for growth.

Vitamin D a chemical substance found in milk and fish liver oils, or obtained by exposure to sunlight on the skin; essential to prevention of rickets and for proper calcium utilization.

vitamins certain kinds of organic chemicals that are needed in small amounts for good health.

whey the fluid which remains after milk has been made into cheese. It is composed of water, lactose, and certain vitamins and minerals.

VIII INDEX TO RECIPES

GENERAL INDEX

ORDER FORM

MEDI-ED PRESS
P.O. Box 957
East Lansing, MI 48826-0957

Please send me_____copy(ies) of *The Milk Sugar Dilemma: Living with Lactose Intolerance* at $13.95 each, plus shipping charges.

I understand that I may return the book for a full refund if I'm not satisfied.

Name_____

Address:_____

_____

_____

Shipping:

_____I'm adding $1.50 for first copy and 50¢ for each additional copy.

_____I can't wait 3-4 weeks for Book Rate. Here is $3.00 per book for Air Mail.

Here are my comments, suggestions and/or criticisms of *The Milk Sugar Dilemma:*

_____

_____

_____

_____

_____

_____

ORDER FORM

MEDI-ED PRESS
P.O. Box 957
East Lansing, MI 48826-0957

Please send me_____ copy(ies) of *The Milk Sugar Dilemma: Living with Lactose Intolerance* at $13.95 each, plus shipping charges.

I understand that I may return the book for a full refund if I'm not satisfied.

Name_____

Address:_____

_____

_____

Shipping:

_____I'm adding $1.50 for first copy and 50¢ for each additional copy.

_____I can't wait 3-4 weeks for Book Rate. Here is $3.00 per book for Air Mail.

Here are my comments, suggestions and/or criticisms of *The Milk Sugar Dilemma:*

_____

_____

_____

_____

_____

_____